Boxy & Me

A Love That Never Died

Kate McNeil
with Chris Berry

GREAT **N** ORTHERN

Great Northern Books
PO Box 1380, Bradford,
West Yorkshire, BD5 5FB

www.greatnorthernbooks.co.uk

ISBN: 978-1-914227-17-2

Design by David Burrill

CIP Data
A catalogue for this book is available from
the British Library

To Andrew

I am only able to do what I do because of your constant love and support

xxx

Contents

Introduction

This is the story of an amazing animal – and how he changed my life. I love musical theatre and Andrew Lloyd Webber's 'Love Never Dies' is my all-time favourite song. It's how I feel about Boxy.

Hallmark Boxster – Boxy – was more than just a bull. It was his spirit, battling through everything thrown at him, that I will always remember with a tear never far from my eyes and a smile in my heart.

Boxy's life was a constant struggle of overcoming massive hurdles. I've had many thrown my way too. Perhaps that was one of the reasons we had such a connection.

I've never experienced the same with any other animal. Our bond was and always will remain very special. I feel him here with me as I write.

Boxy was an outstanding show bull. He never lost. He won at every show he ever appeared and was even triumphant in the High Court in London during our battle with DEFRA.

Through TV appearances he also won the hearts of thousands up and down the country.

He certainly won mine long before all that, and I know I won his.

I still miss him every time I go across to our cattle shed. I loved Boxy while he was alive, and I still love him now.

Okay. Deep breath.

I want to share with you Boxy's remarkable life story from where we left it at the end of the original book *Boxster's Story: The Truth Behind the Bull* and this new book, which now tells his complete story, including his life prior to the events of 2010, a totally updated version of the first book and all of what happened afterwards in our wonderful life with Boxy.

This tells how Boxy became an all-conquering show bull, how he lived out his life after the court ruling meant he didn't have to be destroyed as DEFRA had decreed; and how we, my husband Andrew and I, took on our own farm and started our pedigree herd of British Blonde cattle inspired by this beautiful, incredibull!

In the introduction to the first book, I wrote about our devastation over the initial news that Boxster the Bull was destined to be slaughtered due to what had been recorded as a positive bovine tuberculosis test in 2010. I also told of our frustration in the test having been botched, how DEFRA were intransigent and how we were treated by several DEFRA officials throughout the whole dreadful experience in 2010 and 2011.

Boxster's Story: The Truth Behind the Bull was about setting the record straight; *Boxy & Me: A Love That Never Died* is a celebration of Boxy and where his life has led us today.

Chapter 1

Before Boxy

I was born in 1974. I grew up with my mum and dad, Anita and Ken Jackson, and my elder brother Paul on a farm called Forlorn Hope in the small village of Stubbs Walden. It's roughly in the middle of nowhere, but not far from Pontefract or Doncaster in Yorkshire.

I was what you might call a rough-and-tumble country girl and loved tramping about in my wellies. I'd be with my granddad Les and my dad all the time, getting stuck in and usually ending up very mucky.

I used to go to my granddad's farm at Pollington where he had a poultry unit and one of my first memories is of being hosed down in the garden by my grandma Alice. I'd run up what I thought was a big hill, but it wasn't!

What it happened to be was a mound of chicken poo! I sank in it up to my neck and could have disappeared forever right there and then! Mum and Dad dragged me out before it was too late.

Funny thing today is that I didn't really like hens in those days, but now I'm like, 'Let's have some of those and maybe some of those'. Andrew's like, 'Oh my God, not another chicken house, not more hens!' but now I'm breeding pedigree hens as well as cattle. It must be my granddad's influence.

I've always loved animals. I would play with our nanny goats and used to enjoy looking after the kids.

Being close with animals you form bonds. I remember not really being as much into sheep, but I would feed the pet lambs and there was Charlie who was ace. He was adorable. He'd climb up on my knee, fall asleep in my lap and snore, and even when he was weaned off the bottle he'd still come running over and want a cuddle.

One day my world fell apart. I went off to college in Selby and could see Charlie was there in the paddock, but when I came back, no Charlie. You know what's coming don't you? Dad had taken him away.

Now you might think, being a farmer's daughter, I'd just accept that as a fact of farm life. I did not! This was Charlie! I had a massive tantrum! I screamed, I shouted and cried.

As if that wasn't enough, when I came home from college again a short while later the ultimate situation unfurled. It was teatime, Mum was cooking and Dad said, 'We're having Charlie'. I told him he wasn't at all funny and that I wasn't eating Charlie! But I'm afraid I did. Well, I was hungry. That's life on a farm. My dad making me eat my pet lamb!

While a lot of people know my dad and me because of showing pedigree cattle in cattle rings all around the north of England, that wasn't always the case.

When I was younger Dad had crossbreds and we would have cows that we'd milk for the house. I used to love doing that with him in a morning, milking a Guernsey-cross cow. I remember we would fight over who had the cream off the top.

I was a real cowgirl! I'd ride Dad's cattle up and down our country lane. I was always out and about and up to something.

I used to go to all of the cattle markets with Dad. We went to Selby, Holmfirth, Thirsk and Doncaster.

When I think about it now, in today's very politically correct world, it was a bit mad because I'd be running around a livestock market on my own. I wasn't very old. When Dad had finished buying or selling he'd buy me an ice cream and I'd sit more calmly on the mart steps. I was a real daddy's girl.

As a teenager I studied at Selby College and on a market day I'd meet up with Dad and enjoy a milky coffee in the mart canteen. I've always enjoyed the mart environment.

I started buying calves out of my pocket money, bucket-fed them and sold them on as stores. It was the kind of thing country boys and girls did and still do to make more money.

I don't know quite when I started showing cattle, it's just something I've always done. Growing up in this world it is part of what you do. It's a social day out, a bit of fun and it became my relaxation, most of the time, except when I wasn't occasionally getting peed off with a young handler judge for instance.

Entering the young handler classes is a recognised first step into showing animals. I would usually take part with a crossbred calf, and I won regularly. I knew what I was doing right from the start and I've always been competitive. If you're going to do something you've got to do it right, but I realise you can't always win – unless you were holding Boxy!

Some of my experiences with young handler competitions were bad too. In a regular show competition, where it is all about the animal and not the handler and somebody can tell me why they have placed my animal where they have in the line, then I'll accept it. I may not agree with their decision but everybody's opinion can be different.

But I had one instance as a young handler that topped the lot. I was showing a Belgian Blue X calf which was really extreme. By that I mean it had such muscle and shape. I took it into the ring where there were 15 others and the judge, who never even spoke to me, put me at the end of the line. I was holding a fabulous beast. And I knew everything about it.

I was absolutely fuming! I'd never been put last in my life and I'd taken part in quite a few by then. I could not believe the judge didn't talk to me at all, or from what I could see many others too, apart from those he'd put at the top. It was ludicrous. How are you meant to encourage young people to show cattle if you don't come and talk with them!

That's when I started thinking what I must have done wrong.

It's actually very difficult to pinpoint where you've gone wrong when you've not been spoken to. I just thought, I don't get this. I could see Dad chirruping to everyone about it around the ringside and I just couldn't understand what had happened.

The judge walked out of the ring. He still hadn't bothered to talk to me. Dad went and asked him about what he had just seen. The judge said that it – the calf – had to be one end of the line or the other, that it was too extreme. And that was it. He was judging the calves, not the handlers – well not me, at least. Maybe I needed more lippy on!

A good or even half-decent young handler judge will at very least ask the name of the animal, how old it is, what breed. They're the basics. Fortunately, that experience didn't put me off showing, but it left a nasty taste.

In the years that followed I gradually became more involved with showing Dad's cattle. I never went anywhere for training in prepping them. Dad taught me how to clip. I learned by trial and error. You're generally trying to enhance each animal's assets and cover up anything you don't like. It was a pleasure and a hobby and I'd take time getting it right. We've still got the ancient, heavy blow dryer I used back then.

Brushing the cattle up ready to go into the ring became my thing. I was in charge of prepping and it got to the stage where I wouldn't let Dad touch them because I truly felt I did it better.

I loved showing cattle. Nothing can beat that year I was about to have with Boxy, but when you're leading any animal that you just know is fantastic it gives you that extra spring in your step, that pride.

Dad and I are different in the show ring. He's very laid back. He'll have a chat with people as he's parading around with one of his beasts. He'll chat with those watching as spectators, fellow handlers, anyone.

One of his favourite times was when we used to take part as a breed team against other cattle breeds in 'Housewives Choice' at the Great Yorkshire Show, a fun competition where members of the public decided which breed was their favourite. Dad loved it because he could chat with the women who came into the ring. Chatting them up to get their vote! He knew what he was doing! We won the competition for the breed three times in four years!

Timekeeping in getting to a show wasn't the greatest Jackson trait. We were invariably later than we wanted to be.

We would almost always be late setting off and I knew exactly how long prepping was going to take me doing the hair up, tail, making them shine, getting the head collar on.

Our saviour whenever we arrived was the wonderful Alan Hall, who was Dad's best friend and a fellow British Blonde breeder. He came into his own for us every time. His animals would already be pristine and ready to go in the ring. He'd have our stalls ready, he'd have our trailer door down and have our animals starting to come out before we'd even blinked. Alan would then help me wash them down and get them dry. Whichever one we thought would do best on the day was the one I then concentrated on first. Mum and Dad would soap up the others, which I would then go over before they went in the ring.

I remember one time at a show – I must have been about 15-16 years old – when I had every hair on this beast exactly where I wanted it to be. It was perfect. I can't recall which animal it was, but it was spot on. Then this chap came along and started rubbing its head and back end.

So far as I was concerned all of the last half hour was ruined! I can't remember exactly what I said to him, but I was quite rude! I knew I shouldn't speak out of turn, but he also knew not to touch my animals – or at least he did then!

Getting the animals looking right was one thing. Mum would make sure Dad and I looked right before we went in the show ring. She would put Dad's tie on for him and I'd be brushing a cow's tail up while she'd be brushing my hair or saying I needed a bit of lippy on or that I had a speck of muck on my face. At that time, so long as the animals looked alright, I wasn't bothered if my hair was a mess. It was Mum who stopped me from looking a scruff in the ring.

But I always knew that farming at Forlorn Hope was never going to be my career.

Paul farms it today with Dad and has recently started a butchery and farm shop called The Ranch, which features Boxy on the signage. It's going really well for him and his wife Maria, their daughter Olivia and son Jay.

Farming for me at home was never an option. It's one of those things, but I was always involved with the cattle and showing and I was always helping out, especially if there was a calving involved or help was needed over a caesarean section. I'd shoot over and assist the vet.

I'd originally wanted to become a vet. I had a work placement with Fox Vets at Balby near Doncaster. They were a large and small animal practice and I went along to some big estates, including one near Lincoln where I assisted with dehorning. Some might find that awful, but I absolutely loved it.

For me the realisation of how much study was involved to become a vet – it's seven years – was too much education. I chose physiotherapy instead. I thought it sounded a decent job and it was still about caring.

My husband Andrew and I were best friends for two years at Brayton High School before we became proper boyfriend and girlfriend. We sat together in humanities lessons. I used to mess about in class all the time and he'd do the work and let me copy what he'd done.

We first got together properly at our school leavers party and had our first kiss on the radiator in the main hall. Both our children Patrick and Gemma went to the same school and when parents' evenings took place we always seemed to be sat near it. Andrew and I would nudge each other mentioning 'that radiator'. It's still there, or was the last time they were there. Patrick and Gemma were mortified! We told the school we would buy the radiator if they ever sold it or knocked down the school.

Andrew had decided A levels weren't for him and left school to get a job. I studied a BTEC in healthcare at Selby College and an A level in physics, but my dreams of going to university were dashed by universities prioritising A-level qualifications over BTECs, which were still relatively new. After it happened a second time I gave up hoping I would be accepted. My work placements had taken me to the burns unit in Pinderfields, Wakefield and Stanley Royd Hospital.

You will see where all this is heading very soon – and how in a roundabout way I ended up doing a job that was to stand me in good stead for what was to happen to Boxy years later.

Having given up hope of my university studies I took a job in Doncaster Royal Infirmary. I started as a lab assistant in the laboratories. I was separating blood samples!

That's right, separating bloody blood samples! Can you believe it!

Blood, in a sealed vial. Let's re-emphasise that. A sealed vial.

It was about processing the vials for analysis. You get the blood in the sealed vial, it gets put into a machine and is spun until it separates so that the clear blood can be tested.

That was my job for two years before a job came up in theatre. It was a role called Operating Department Practitioner (ODP) with training on the job over two years in theatre with surgeons.

The role also involved working with the anaesthetist. It means you learn to multi-task. You're either involved with the ventilator, providing air; sedation, keeping patients asleep; or you're passing instruments and taking instructions from the surgeons. You are involved in everything from major surgery in theatre to any medical emergency that may occur anywhere in the hospital and the most important things are to keep a clear head and listen intently to your surgeon.

I was an ODP for over a decade, quite a long time. I was promoted and took a senior role as a lead practitioner.

My career took an important turn when a consultant anaesthetist and a consultant surgeon both called Alistair began developing a simulation centre that was all about how surgeons, anaesthetists, GPs, dental practices, and intensive care professionals managed their teams to achieve the best outcome for the patients. They had their own emergency scenario and mannequin.

The two Alistairs opened up this training centre in Mexborough and invited me to join them. It was roleplay, offering practitioners the opportunity to develop their leadership of teams. It is all well and good being the best consultant in the world, but you also need to know how to manage people or communicate properly – and those who work with you need to know what is required of them too.

Everything was filmed and played back for debriefing.

I would assist in the scenarios to make them lifelike. Often these very knowledgeable, highly trained and incredibly talented people would start off quite hostile. It wasn't real, after all. But then they would mellow and by the end of the day there was respect for the opportunity to learn. I undertook a teaching qualification and began running my own courses.

I don't think I would have dared take on any of Boxy's case if it hadn't been for that medical knowledge, particularly early on when dealing with blood samples. I one hundred per cent believe that the confidence I gained through scenario-based training, with people far more knowledgeable than I will ever be, was what gave me the confidence to take on DEFRA.

We were informed along the way that people in DEFRA were talking about me in emails. I understand they started getting anxious. They had picked up on my background and I recall hearing someone say that because of the questions I was asking I sounded very knowledgeable. They thought I might be a nurse. That's what I heard.

I don't think DEFRA knew what hit them when they realised they weren't up against some crazy woman, but someone who actually understood the process of blood sampling. Maybe a little bit crazy too, but always well intentioned for the sake of Boxy – the bull that lives on in my heart and will do forever!

Chapter 2

Boxy &
the Perfect Show Season

Hallmark Boxster was born 7 October 2006. His pedigree as a Blonde d'Aquitaine bull came from sire Whistley Dollar and cow Stocksfield Imagination. We showed him for just one glorious, imperious season in 2009. It sounds strange now, given all that happened, but before we started showing that year Boxy really was just another bull.

He made his show debut at the Nottinghamshire County Show at Newark in May 2009 and finished his season and, as it turned out, his show career at Nidderdale Show in Pateley Bridge in September. He was breed champion and male junior champion at the Great Yorkshire Show in Harrogate. It was the perfect show season. He was undefeated in the ring at seven major agricultural shows and we were looking forward to carrying on that trend in 2010.

It was fantastic for Dad. He and Mum were so proud. We all were. Showing pedigree cattle is a fulfilling, enjoyable hobby as well as a great shop window for your breed, especially when you have one as amazing as Boxy. There are not many hobbies that can tick the boxes of good business – when you get the right animal – involve the whole family and bring you friendships that last a lifetime. Dad has always loved the social side. He's chatty, friendly, loves people and they love him.

He had started with what are now called British Blondes when the Blonde d'Aquitaine breed from France was still relatively new to this country quite a few years ago. He had built up a strong reputation for the quality of his herd and Boxy was his pot of gold at the end of the rainbow.

Dad and I generally found that certain animals took better to either him or me, which usually happened when we began working with them as young animals to join our show team.

I can't honestly remember that exact moment of realisation when that happened with Boxy, he just went well for me and was such an easy animal to show. Many show people talk of their great cattle, sheep and horses as having that sense of enjoying being on show. Boxy always had that same aura about him. He knew he was star quality.

What was strange when Dad and I worked together was that the bulls tended to take to me and the heifers to him. I never worked out why. It was just the way it was. The young bulls were always my babies and I liked it like that.

I loved taking a big, impressive, powerful bull into the ring and also loved showing the public just how friendly such a large animal can be. I would get people to stroke them and sometimes lie with them.

Boxy was such a good-natured bull and he would do everything I asked of him. Children would sit on him and ladies who were visiting the shows would kiss him. He was just so placid.

As the season went on and the trophies kept coming, I began spending more and more time with him and we just built up this thing between us. I'd take time over clipping, talk with him affectionately and he just knew he was loved.

Trust is vital in building the bond between handlers and animals. It's obviously pretty important from person to person, but when you're dealing with an animal that can't talk to let you know how it feels then trust is everything.

Boxy's show season was immaculate, but he didn't have things easy even then. We were well into the season and he began to suffer with his eyes. I was concerned for him.

He'd started with a runny eye and our vet had given us

some cream. Unfortunately, that only appeared to make matters worse. He became so swollen around the eye that he couldn't see. An injection was tried but his eye kept on getting worse and then his other eye started playing up as well. He looked more like a boxer than Boxster.

There were times when his eyes were streaming with water and he would keep them shut tight. We tried him on a number of types of medication to try and sort it out. His eyes would clear up a little, then something would seem to trigger it and he would start all over again. When the vets injected him he was so well behaved.

We still competed at shows despite his eye problem. It must have been around the time of our heaviest run of shows.

He would be alright when we set off from the farm, but then his eyes would start running and they would swell up again. This is when Boxy and I made our relationship complete. I felt for him so much and what he must be going through. He'd be in a pen on his own, but still in the barn with the rest of the herd. I would talk with him and encourage him, tell him I would look after him. I'd go in and brush him, sit with him and sometimes lead him around the pen. I made a fuss over him.

I would constantly talk to him as we were walking around the show ring. I'd just keep my voice calm and do all I could to make sure he felt safe and secure. He listened and if I told him to go steady he would do just that. I talked him through several shows and we still won them all.

While he'd had his runny eyes he had learned to trust me implicitly. I led him around the farm and spent hours just talking to him, giving him reassurance. He was so good and behaved like a perfect gentleman. And he was ready for the biggest show he would ever compete at for the biggest title in the agricultural show calendar.

The Great Yorkshire Show at Harrogate is my favourite of them all. I absolutely love it and it's the one where I always want to do my very best. Andrew and I have had success there ourselves since starting out on our own, but this was Boxy's year and he swept the board. It was a triumph for us all. A perfect moment with a very nearly perfect bull, apart from a runny eye.

During this time when Boxy's eye problem had become really bad, and after having tried various creams and injections, we took him to an eye specialist at an equine hospital, which is part of our vet's practice. The specialist was more used to dealing with eye problems in horses and dogs, but we weren't bothered about that. He was an eye specialist in animals and we just wanted to make progress.

The specialist was able to start getting Boxy back on the right track straight away. He explained that Boxy's eyes were swelling up because he was squeezing them so tightly and that was causing the runniness. That wouldn't have been so bad, but it turned out that his eyelids were rolling over and his eyelashes were scratching his eyeballs. Boxy seemed to have become caught up in a vicious circle where one thing was causing another.

Boxy ended up having an operation called an entropion, where his eyelids were stitched closed. Our bond during this time was to become even stronger, especially with what happened next.

When he was about to have his operation I led him into the stall at the veterinary practice, Bishopton Vets in Ripon. The specialist told us that he was going to sedate him and give him something to take the edge off what he was doing.

After Boxy's sedation all the lights were turned off because they wanted him quiet and felt that being in the dark was best. Somebody had to stay with him. I bet you can't guess who that was!

My dad said it would be best if it was, 'Our Kate. He trusts her.' So, I stayed there, in the dark, in this room and I cuddled him.

When they shut the doors was when I suddenly began to realise how dangerous this could be if it all went wrong.

I was in the pitch black with this massive three-year-old bull. He was a big lad, and he'd just been given some sort of medication. Who knows how it might have turned out if he'd had some kind of reaction that sent him crazy!

What made it worse was that I could hear them all talking outside. I was talking with Boxy, trying to soothe him, whispering softly to him. His head was getting heavier as the sedation took hold and he was starting to snore a little.

That's when I heard my dad say, 'So what will happen next?' Then another voice, I think it was the specialist, replied: 'I'm not right sure how he'll react. He could go one way or the other.' My uncle Henry was there with Dad and I heard him say, 'You should get Kate out of there.'

What!! Suddenly I was thinking, 'Oh my God! They're all out there and I'm in here and they don't even know whether he might flip his lid!' I started talking to him a lot more after that. By now I had his head in my arms, which was getting heavier and heavier.

I needn't have worried.

Boxy became very drowsy, they came to conduct the operation, his eyelids were stitched closed and he took about a month to recover, in between shows. It was like he was a sportsman who had an injury but hadn't a competitive match to play while he recuperated.

I was looking forward to the 2010 show season when Boxy would be competing for the first time as a mature bull. We were confident that he could continue his majestic record and it was going to be some year. He knew what he was doing in the show ring, we worked so well together, he was getting bigger, even stronger and looked fabulous. Nobody had been able to touch us in 2009 and I couldn't see any way that any animal could beat him. I really do believe Boxy was looking forward to it too.

Sadly, all of those high hopes were never to turn into reality. Little did we know that as we finished our show season in September 2009 that Boxy would not be able to compete at all the following year – and for Hallmark Boxster, champion bull of 2009, his showing days were already over.

Chapter 3

The Routine Test
That Changed Everything

12 March 2010 was when it all started. It was just two months before the new show season. My world collapsed.

Every four years we had a routine bovine TB test. I'd grown up with that. It was just something that happened, nothing unusual. All farms with cattle are tested. It depends on which area you are in as to how often these routine tests take place. If you're in a high-risk area – where incidences of bovine TB are more prevalent – your cattle are tested more frequently. If you're in a low-risk area it is once every four years.

We knew that bovine TB cases had occurred further north, having originally been concentrated in the south-west of England. Like every other cattle farming operation, we had our fingers crossed that all would be okay and that it would be another four years before Dad's herd would be tested again.

That morning of 12 March, we weren't unduly concerned about the test. We hadn't had any problems with our animals. They were all in great shape.

Becky arrived from Bishopton Vets. We knew her pretty well as she came regularly. Everyone was relaxed, everything was normal. It was around mid-morning, the day was cold and overcast which, unbeknown to us at the time, was exactly how we would feel three days later!

When you have a routine test you don't necessarily put all of the cattle through. All we were putting through that day were the breeding cattle, because the concern is usually over those animals that may move on to another farm.

That meant the cattle destined for the beef meat trade, the fat cattle, didn't take the test. There is little interest in testing them because of the minimal possibility of contact they will have with other livestock.

The routine test is a skin test. What happens is that a small area of the neck is shaved to mark where the injections will take place. The size of the shaved area depends on who is doing it. It's a clip-mark so that the person who is conducting the test knows where the injection has been. It's usually around the mid-neck where it is fleshy. Whether it is shaved on the right or left side of the neck doesn't make a difference, it is actually more dependent on your cattle crush (a strongly built stall or cage for holding cattle still and safe whilst examining or administering treatment takes place) and how it is situated. Generally, the shaved area on each of our cattle had been on the right side.

Each animal has its skin thickness measured using callipers. This is carried out by the person who has come on to your farm, prior to that same person injecting a small amount of bovine TB into the animal. They inject both avian TB and bovine TB, with the avian TB injected above the bovine TB.

There is then a three-day term between the injection being administered and a second measurement of the skin, with the same callipers. The test is looking for the body's reaction to that small amount of TB having been injected.

Injections are administered using a preloaded syringe in a gun. The needle is no more than a couple of millimetres long, so it doesn't penetrate deeply. The gun is put against the neck, the trigger is pulled and it shoots 0.1 milligrams of bovine TB into the skin. The operator has a holster with two guns, one for the administering of the avian TB and one for the bovine TB.

From what I had read, the needles are supposed to be changed, according to protocol, every 20 injections because they will start to go blunt. However, I've never seen anyone change a needle.

The size of the reaction to the bovine TB injection is what matters. If there is no reaction at all the skin will be flat after three days, but any lump that has increased the skin measurement by over five millimetres is deemed as a positive reactor and that's when you start getting worried.

We had no real idea what it meant to have a reactor. We'd never had one. We'd heard of others having them but we didn't know how that dreadful news would impact on our lives for the next two years. Our nightmare was just about to start.

There was no cause for concern. We were just going through the motions of another four-yearly test. It would be over, we would pass with no problem and on we would go for another four years. You never count your chickens, as the saying goes, but we honestly couldn't see this as being a problem.

Everyone has their own role on the farm when these tests take place. Paul and the lads who work with him feed the cattle into the crush area. Mum looks after all the paperwork so that it's all in order. Dad shuts the gates and puts the bars behind them in the crush.

My role was to stand at the head so I could see everything that's happening, then release them out of the crush.

We put around 35 cattle through that day, taking a couple of hours. The show cattle were first because they were easier to handle as they were used to being led. They didn't go through the cattle crush.

They are big, powerful animals and we didn't want to risk them getting stuck and doing damage to themselves. We tied them up and Becky got on with the test.

We had also tied up the grandma of them all, Nectarine, who was 14 years old and had been another of our top show animals some years ago. Whilst we kept the others out of the crush, because of their size, we simply didn't want her getting bashed about by the other cattle.

Every pedigree animal over six months old went through, including all of our young breeding bulls, around 15 of them. Boxy went through.

It was a happy day. We drank coffee, infused with Dad's favourite Famous Grouse whisky, purely to keep off the cold of course, and ate some cake.

We were totally oblivious to the fact that our very own 'annus horribilis' was about to begin.

Chapter 4

Three Days Later
Our Troubles Began

Becky came back three days later to conduct the skin measurements. We truly had no thought of how our life was about to be blown apart in the next sixty minutes.

It was my birthday. Mum and I had been planning on going off shopping and having a meal.

We knew that this part of the test was much quicker because all Becky had to do was use her callipers. Becky had arrived around nine o'clock that morning and all we were thinking was right, let's get this over with and off we go for the day.

There was never a single thought about what was to come. We'd never had a problem. We had thought it would be all over in an hour.

Mum and I never went shopping that day. It really was all over in an hour, but in a far different way than we could ever have imagined.

We sent the cattle through the crush again. We tied up those that we had tied up previously. We were all laughing and joking. Mum and I were looking forward to our day out. There were no worries.

My dad always looks around the cattle conducting his normal checks. He thought everything was okay. He wasn't really looking or feeling for lumps though because we'd never had a problem.

The vet ran her hand over all of the stock. It's as simple a check as that. She then measured the thickness of the skin again with her callipers and documented any changes, using the ear tag number to identify the animal.

The last animal we put through that day was Stubbs Walden Carol. We named her after Carol Hall, Alan's wife. She was also a great friend and a very feisty lady. Sadly, Alan and Carol both passed away some time ago now. Stubbs Walden Carol was headstrong just like Carol Hall.

After 34 of the 35 animals had passed their skin test with flying colours the vet took out her callipers for Carol.

We could all see there was a lump, but we didn't know what it meant to us at that point. How it changed everything. You don't really know until it happens to your animals.

I don't think any of us took any real notice of what Becky was doing. I just thought she was writing up her notes. I was convinced she was just signing off on the herd and we were done for another four years. That was it – Mum and I were ready for some retail therapy.

Becky's words changed everything. She said:

'I'm sorry Ken, I think this is a reactor.'

My dad's exact words were: 'Oh, bloody 'ell, what's that mean?'

None of us knew what it meant at that moment, although I'm sure Mum and Dad knew it couldn't mean anything but bad news. They'd had more than their fair share of that in recent times.

I don't think I thought or felt anything just at that moment, apart from a feeling of numbness. I certainly didn't understand the implications it would have for the farm or our lives in the coming years. I'm sure none of us ever dreamed where it would lead us.

Becky was as shocked as we were. She checked again. She was pretty sure.

We went up to the house and Becky phoned the news in to the surgery. We sat and had a drink whilst she explained what she had found. She was very apologetic and told us she felt really bad. I think she knew what it might mean.

We still didn't have a clue. We were all just in a state of shock.

Becky said that someone from Animal Health would contact us and that we would be assigned a vet who would visit and tell us what we needed to do. Our first job was to keep Carol separate from the herd. We moved her immediately.

Making that move, isolating one of our herd, started to bring us round to what we were facing.

As we sat back down around the living room you could see the worry in all our faces and the way we were behaving. Dad was slumped in an armchair, looking drained. Mum was flitting between the kitchen and the living room trying to keep moving. I was sitting there in total shock.

Becky stayed with us for an hour or so after giving us the bad news. She left around 1.30pm. It was a good deal later than we had been anticipating. Our proposed shopping trip was already a distant memory.

Once Becky had gone the house was so quiet. We were all subdued. I think we were all very worried. No-one wanted to talk about it. We didn't know what to say or how to behave. We all just feared the worst. We knew about things like movement restrictions that would automatically be imposed on our herd.

Chapter 5

First Thoughts

Following Becky's pronouncement that day, my own first, purely selfish, thoughts were that we wouldn't be able to compete at the agricultural shows that year.

Boxy not being able to replicate his success at the Great Yorkshire Show and everywhere else was heartbreaking for me, but then I knew only too well this would all run a lot deeper and would have a massive impact on the farm. My dad and Paul's business. Their livelihood.

Prior to our first visit from a vet from Animal Health I prepared myself.

I like to know what I'm getting involved with before I go into a meeting and to be armed with at least some knowledge.

Through my job I was teaching management of medical emergencies to NHS staff at Montagu Hospital in Mexborough. This was now our very own emergency and I fully intended to manage it as best I could.

Medically, I had acquired quite a bit of knowledge and having worked in laboratories I knew a bit about blood samples. Although we didn't know it at the time, it was these experiences that were going to help in our battle.

It was the crisis management side of my job that helped me to start thinking of how we could at the very least be geared up for that first visit. The type of job I was involved with at the time had taught me not to be intimidated by people, no matter how important they might be, or in some cases might feel they were.

By the time we received our first visit from Crispin Madavo, of Animal Health, I had conducted as much research as I could.

I'd been on the DEFRA website and checked out their advice on what you should do if you have a reactor in your herd.

I didn't look up what others had done at that time, but I knew that the herd would be on complete shutdown for at least a few months. The whole herd would now have to undergo two more 100 per cent clear skin tests before being given the all-clear. I knew that we were effectively quarantined for at least 120 days.

If you calculate from when Becky found that Carol was a reactor on 15 March 2010 and add up the number of days until the first day of the Great Yorkshire Show that year, being Tuesday 13 July, guess what? It was exactly 120 days.

Surely, we couldn't be that lucky could we? It would be an absolute miracle if we were to make it – and we'd definitely need Alan's (Alan Hall) help, as all cattle are usually on the showground the day before the Great Yorkshire starts.

Even if I'd held out this last hope in any way it was going to be more than quashed in the coming days and weeks. This was a very real, living nightmare. And at this point we were not even at the stage where Boxy was under threat of being destroyed. All that was to come.

Chapter 6

Animal Health's First Visit

When Crispin Madavo arrived on our farm for the first time on 19 March 2010 we held no resentment towards Animal Health as an organisation.

Perhaps naively, we felt that Animal Health was there to support and work together with farmers. We had no issue with the test which had been completed and which found Carol to be a reactor.

We were concerned for the farm's future. We had no idea just how little the Animal Health staff would try to help us and how their strict adherence to 'policy' almost destroyed everything Mum, Dad and Paul had worked hard to achieve.

That doesn't mean we ended up thinking everyone from Animal Health was a bad 'un, but what happened in the months that followed left a very bad taste.

My first impression of Crispin Madavo was that he was very official. I'd never known us have anyone turn up like him before.

It was always quite laid back and friendly at Forlorn Hope, very matter-of-fact, no airs and graces.

Here we had a man with his clipboard and protective overalls like forensic scientists wear.

We'd had plenty of vets diligently washing their boots before coming onto the farm, but this felt different.

We're not stupid. We knew that by having a reactor and then having a visit from an Animal Health representative this was serious, but we were also used to a friendly, co-operative attitude and I can't say we felt that from him. We were made to feel as though our farm was a leper colony.

He took a look around the herd and confirmed what we had already feared, that the heifer Carol would have to be slaughtered. He told us that his department would arrange the paperwork so that we could take her to the slaughterhouse and that the farm was now on shut-down, that nothing could move from the farm unless it was going to slaughter. He wandered around making lots of notes.

Once he had finished looking around the herd we all went into the house and that's when our situation finally hit home.

He explained the process of what was to happen. He told us that Animal Health would come to skin test every bull and heifer on the farm that was over six weeks old.

'Why everything?' said Dad. 'Why the commercial cattle as well as the Blondes?'

Dad had thought that since Carol was one of the pedigree herd and we had kept her separate from the commercial cattle it was purely the Blondes that would need testing.

But cross-contamination could occur. The commercials weren't mixed with the Blondes as such, but there were ways in which they could have nose-to-nose contact, which is how the disease can be passed on through the herd.

Bovine TB is transmitted through body fluids and respiratory tracts. We were also using the same bucket on the tractor to feed both the pedigrees and the non-pedigrees. That could also have been a contributory factor.

We had never thought about things this way before because we'd never had a problem. Now we were learning fast.

We spoke about the show team, which at that moment was made up of just Boxster and Katie.

We generally kept the show team separate from the rest of the Blondes as they are fed a different ration, and also because we had always been aware that the more times you take animals out amongst others and bring them back on farm you were increasing the potential for bringing back disease.

Most farms keep their show teams separate for the same

reasons.

Crispin Madavo told us that if they were isolated from the rest of the Blondes, as they already were, we could apply for them to be listed as a separate herd.

It would mean that they would need to pass another skin test and then restrictions would be lifted on them as long as they were kept in an approved quarantine area. That way we could still show them. He said we could draw up plans. The pen would need to be organised to his specification, ensuring that they were an appropriate distance away from the rest to avoid contact via saliva, sneezing or coughing.

This, to me, was a glimmer of hope, a little light at the end of our tunnel. But even that little light didn't last long.

We had to tell Crispin everything about where we bought cattle and where we had moved them. It was then that we felt a bit like the farmer in Northumberland must have felt in 2001 when it turned out he was blamed for the start of foot-and mouth-disease.

Crispin Madavo scribbled everything down, documenting what we were telling him, and trying to build up a picture of where the bovine TB may have come from. That's part of the Animal Health role, tracing where things have come from.

It's why most farmers today hold the word traceability in high esteem. Farmers are now much more conscious, when buying stock elsewhere, of where it has come from and ensuring that they have what is called high health status. That's why cattle passports are now so important. Everything is traceable today.

We gave this man as much information as we could, because we now wanted to know where the bovine TB had come from.

There was one thought. Our commercial herd was made up of crossbred bull calves bought from a farm in West Yorkshire. Dad had bought them from the same farmer for a number of years.

We would get them from him at a few days old, usually in batches of at least half a dozen at a time. It's a system a lot of dairy farmers operate. They sell the calves their cows produce when they are young and commercial beef cattle farmers like Dad buy them to take them through to beef.

The chap who Dad was buying them from hadn't had a reactor when he'd been routinely tested, but we found out in the course of our later research that his neighbour had, but the same neighbour's farm had been given the all-clear six months previously so it appeared unlikely that it could have come from there.

This was the only farm we bought any cattle from. The only place where it would have been possible that we may have picked up something that would link back to a possible bovine TB case. Or so we thought.

We then remembered that we had taken Carol to Carlisle for a breed sale, but she hadn't made the reserve price, so we had brought her home and decided to breed with her. She had only just given birth to a calf when she had been deemed to have tested positive for bovine TB. Maybe she had picked it up from cattle at Carlisle?

There was also the possibility that any disease could have come from wildlife. There are a lot of badgers and deer close to the farm and everyone knows just how much talk there is of badgers being bovine TB carriers.

As Crispin Madavo talked about the possibilities of how the disease may have got onto the farm, it then came over me like an all-consuming black cloud that we could have even more reactors.

We had only had 35 animals tested and we had around 180 cattle on the farm at that time. This shocked me even more than previously and I was beginning to frighten myself over what might happen to the farm, my mum and dad, Paul, his family. Boxy wasn't my number one priority just at that moment. I was getting seriously worried.

The plight of the farm and everything that might be at risk became even more daunting the more Crispin spoke. The things he was saying, the timescale he was talking about and the sources the bovine TB could have come from made me think that we could lose all of our cattle.

And there was another frightening thought.

I don't think it had ever entered our heads that we might have put anyone else at risk, but now I could see how that might have been possible. I could see how farmers and farming families could easily become distressed and feel sick inside that they and we might be the cause of someone else's misfortune.

The Blondes were a closed herd, which meant we didn't buy cattle in as a rule, but we do go on and off farm with them during show season. And we do sell them to other farms. Maybe our actions were what had brought it about or could be responsible for others' future problems. The capacity for disease transmission was now in the front of our minds.

Carol was one of the pedigree herd. She had been with the rest of the herd. The implications of that didn't bear thinking about, but that was exactly what we had to do. Think about it hard.

It was then that we all started thinking that Carol's positive reaction to the bovine TB test might not be the only case we had in the herd.

Up until that point we were thinking about it as to why the disease had come and why specifically Carol.

By now I was totally beside myself for the implications this had for the whole herd.

I was trying to stay on the same wavelength as Crispin Madavo, to listen intently to his instructions and show that we understood what needed to be done.

The one thing we could do was to run the farm the way he wanted it to be, from a sterility and clinical point of view.

But there were concerns too.

There was the farm itself and also the woodchip business. The woodchip started in 1999 and had built up steadily. Paul was making a couple of very popular products – Stable-Dry, which was a dust-free product that he bagged and sold to stables for horse bedding; and a thicker product that was delivered in bulk loads for cattle bedding.

Paul and his team were making regular deliveries to farms and stables throughout Yorkshire and further afield. He was obviously very concerned about his trade, but also what other farms would think about receiving his bedding from us.

We were aware that during the time of foot-and-mouth disease there had been a lot of talk about disease being transmitted from trucks' wheels. If the farm was to lose the woodchip trade and only be able to sell cattle by going direct to slaughter the farm finances would soon become severely stretched.

The whole family's emotions were all over the place. We now also felt guilty, like a lot of others must feel when they find out they have a reactor, because we could have passed on disease to other farms.

All we wanted to do was the right thing, to make sure that everything was back to normal as quickly as it could be.

Dad was very worried, but typically not for himself but for others. He had just sold three breeding bulls from the Blonde herd. They had been sold to three individual farms. One had gone to a farmer who had a herd of 500 dairy cows. The look on Dad's face as he told Crispin about this brought tears to my eyes.

Mum and Dad have always thought about everyone else before themselves and here they were again worrying themselves sick that they may have inadvertently caused pain and heartache to others.

Dad told Crispin that he'd only taken one of the bulls to its new owner a couple of weeks before the skin test. He asked Crispin whether we should phone the three farms so that they could isolate the bulls just in case, but Crispin told us that Animal Health would trace all of the animals we had told him about.

Once Crispin had gone I couldn't hold in my emotions any longer. I'd tried to appear tough as old boots in front of him, but I was so worried now about everything. Dad gave me a hug and told me it was going to be alright.

I wasn't as worried about Boxy because it felt as though we had shielded him by finding out that we could set up a separate herd.

How wrong was I!

Chapter 7

Letting Others Know

'As soon as we had that first reactor I felt the farm was now dirty. I hoped we hadn't passed on the disease to anybody. Then you go into a bit of panic about it. We'd had the fear of god put into us. Ken and I talked about it and we rang all our neighbours who we knew had cattle. We also rang the people we had sold bulls to. We were trying to do what we could, but we didn't realise what lay ahead of us.'

Anita Jackson

'We'd had these four-yearly tests a few times and had never had a reactor. That's why we weren't concerned when the vet came in March 2010. I don't think it really sunk in to me just what a reactor really was until we had one. I didn't know what it entailed. No-one in this area had ever had one before.

'When we got the confirmation that the farm was going to be closed down my first reaction was that it was going to stop us showing for a while. We didn't know how long but that was what hit me. Showing our cattle is such a big part of our life and it's where we all really enjoy ourselves. The cattle were already in show condition. Through the summer we go to at least one show every week from the little ones to the county shows.

'Not being able to sell any livestock was the other thing. I had just decided to go all pedigree with the herd before this started and I was gradually cutting down on the commercial herd.

'I was worried about the three farmers who had recently bought bulls from us. Crispin had said we didn't have to contact them, that his people would do it, but that didn't seem right to me. I wanted to

contact them as soon as possible. If it had been me in their position, I would have wanted to know straight away so that I could separate them from the herd and limit any damage. So that's what I did. I rang them that same day.'

   Ken Jackson

'When Crispin came out and told us about the farm being on shut-down I was very concerned. I didn't know how it would affect our delivery of wood chip to farms. The bedding was a big part of the overall business and it worried me that we would be stopped from taking it from here. We put in all the precautions. Initially I felt panic. This seemed to be another foot-and-mouth disease time. I found out that the strength of the disinfectant had to be three times greater than we used at that time.'

   Paul Jackson

That's how Mum, Dad and Paul felt and what they did. The reactions received from the three farmers and our neighbours who had cattle were supportive. It was mostly along the lines of, 'Oh bloody 'ell, that's awful', rather than, 'My god, what have you sold us!'

Everybody buys stock in, especially in our area, and people didn't really understand what bovine TB meant. We were all about to understand it from then on.

Chapter 8

Disinfectant Days

Boxster and Katie were moved to an isolation pen, basically their own little field, within a few days of Crispin's visit. He hadn't thought that our idea of isolating them in a separate barn, which was attached to the main cattle shed, was appropriate. He reckoned that doing this would have continued offering opportunity for disease to be passed on.

Paul built the isolation pen. It had no cover for either Boxster or Katie. We were at the end of March 2010. It wasn't winter, but it was still cold and horrible at times. Where it succeeded was that at least they were now both far enough from the rest of the herd and, even more importantly, Crispin had agreed to it.

Our next date with destiny was set to take place on 2 April. This was the date when the whole of the herd would have a skin test. I made sure I was available and spent the next two weeks busying myself, trying to get us ahead of the game, conducting as much research as I could.

The first thing I made sure of was that the farm and Paul's business were following every health guideline possible. I know Paul was worried about whether Animal Health would stop him going on to other farms and stables. We were all concerned about that. We made sure that the appropriate disinfectant was administered all around the farm.

'We had such a job getting hold of the right disinfectant. Animal Health couldn't get the stuff either. In the end a friend of ours, Phillip Holden managed to track it down.'

Paul Jackson

We had disinfectant hand washes and foot washes. We put carpets down soaked in disinfectant for the vehicles. We made sure the wheels of the wagons carrying the bedding were sprayed as they were going out and coming back in. The bedding that we used on-farm was kept completely separate to the bedding that was being sold. That way there could be no cross-contamination possibility.

I wrote a protocol for all the lads and made them sign it. I laminated the sheet and put it up all around the farm so that nobody could be in any doubt about what they had to do. They had to take off all their work clothes and work boots and leave them on the farm when they left, going home in completely different clothes. It just felt so important that we were doing everything in our power to ensure that the disease couldn't enter or be transported.

I had gone back to what farmers had done during foot-and-mouth disease in 2001. My medical background was a help. It's important for me to say that all of the procedures we had put in place were our own. We were given no regulations from Animal Health. So far as they were concerned the farm was shut down and that was it.

More bad news was to follow.

Four days after Crispin had visited the farm we received a letter stating that a blood test of the whole herd was now required.

Carol had been destroyed by then and lesions had been found on her at post-mortem.

Animal Health examined the carcass and made their report. We will never know how many they found, but we were told that there was at least one lesion in her lymph node, in her neck.

When I became more on-the-ball over listening to every

word Animal Health were saying in the months that followed, I believe they either referred to this either as a single lesion or in plural terminology at different times, but at that particular moment we were still in too much of a state of shock to let it register.

The news of a lesion or lesions being found, whether singular or plural, wasn't quite a hammer blow to me at the time, because we had blithely accepted the fact that she had bovine TB.

We were still numb and were just trying to go along with what we were being told by the authorities.

A blood test was set for five days after the second skin test. We now had two hurdles to get over, so even if our cattle passed the second skin test we knew that we wouldn't rest easy with the blood test to follow.

There was one bright spot along the way.

The day after we received the blood test letter, we received permission for Boxster and Katie to become a separate herd as Crispin had suggested.

We weren't euphoric, but it gave us some comfort that if they both passed the blood test and a second skin test we could show them in the summer that was fast approaching.

As it turned out, our summer was over before it had begun.

Chapter 9

The Second Skin Test

It had been three weeks since our first skin test. We had done all we could in that time to limit the chances of having another reactor, but no matter how much we had tried to get on with a normal life it was impossible.

Looking back, there was so much we still didn't know. We were simply accepting our fate. We were unlucky. That's how it seemed.

This time it was the Animal Health people who came to the farm. They had taken over from our vets. It was the same rigmarole as it had been with the earlier skin test. The necks were shaved, the injections of bovine TB were administered.

It took hours as the whole of the herd, apart from those who had been tested three weeks prior, was put through this time.

The rules had also changed in the respect that now everything over six weeks old (it had been everything over six months old at the first test) that hadn't been tested the first time received their dosage from the little calves to the big bulls. There were the young pedigree Blondes and all of the commercials, 88 animals in total. We started around ten o'clock in the morning and finished at nearly three o'clock.

Nobody really said anything. Our hearts were well and truly in our mouths, and we were all silently praying and hoping that this would be the first step on our way to the farm having its shutdown notice lifted. We just wanted to be back where we had been before the results of 12 March.

What we also didn't know at the time was that a number of

the rules change once you've had one reactor. In fact, everything is different. It's like everything is ramped up.

Three days later, just as Becky had done previously, Animal Health returned with their callipers.

During those three days we had all been checking the herd, looking to see whether we could notice any lumps. Mum, Dad, Paul and me, and being perfectly honest, we thought some were showing signs of lumps, but when you're in the kind of state we'd now got to you can convince yourself of anything.

If you're pessimistic you think everything will have a lump, if you're an optimist you try to imagine that the lump isn't as big as you really think. In short, we were now panicking like mad.

Our hope was that the reactor we'd had (Carol) was a one-off, but our hopes were soon to be dashed.

We were on tenterhooks as each animal was put through. Paul was getting them loaded into the holding area for the race that leads up to the crush. Every time one came into the crush, I was standing at its head watching the measurements being taken and reading the ear tags.

When Animal Health had taken the measurement and I could see it was okay I would look at Paul and give him another nod. There was a lot of eye contact going on and after each animal was successful in being checked and was in the clear there was a sigh of relief.

One by one the animals were getting put through the crush and then one little calf, around five months old, measured positive as a reactor.

Our hearts sank. We were all devastated. It was over. All we had done to try and avert this situation had been to no avail.

We had hoped against hope that in some way we had suffered one isolated incident and this test would prove we were now back on the straight and narrow. We were in trouble.

Even worse, the calf that had reacted was a commercial. It had been nowhere near the pedigrees. If we had been expecting anything being a reactor, we would have thought that we would have had one from the Blondes, as that was where we had the one earlier. But this calf had been at the other side of the yard to Carol.

The saving grace, if you can call it that, was that this was the only reactor we had that day. We isolated the calf immediately and left him there until we received notification to take him to slaughter.

What we didn't know at the time was that when you have had a confirmed reactor in your herd they make the regulations tighter.

We speculated that this was because they are perhaps trying to catch cattle in the early stages, but we were shocked by the gauge they work by.

When you have not had a reactor, as we hadn't before the test in March, the benchmark remains at a five-millimetre increase to the thickness of skin during the three days since the TB injection. The minute you've had a reactor the thickness of skin has to have been increased by just two millimetres in the three days. It's hardly more than a pimple! Any animal can get a lump from purely getting a knock or rubbing its neck against something.

If we had been aware of the stricter regulations at the time we may have challenged the test, perhaps asked for the measurement to be checked again. But we weren't – and we didn't.

If we had still been on the five-millimetre ruling, we may have been in the clear. We will never know. But even at the much stricter two millimetres we'd still only had one reactor from that 88.

Of course, having one was enough but if we had asked Animal Health to check again who knows what the result would have been.

Right then we were still in the foothills of the mountain we were about to climb. And it was to be an exhausting journey.

We had no game plan in those early days because we didn't see things in that way. We were, probably like most farmers would be, a little naïve to the whole testing procedure and just let the officials get on with it.

In retrospect, I of all people should have known to have asked questions and double-checked what they were doing at every stage, because I had first-hand experience of professional, talented people getting things wrong in my simulation work. I'm not saying they got it wrong over the calf, but we weren't in the right frame of mind to question what was happening at that stage.

That's one of the reasons why we were so keen to write this book the first time around, to help others understand what we went through.

We were trying desperately hard not to get paranoid at this point, but it was getting harder to remain optimistic because we were also realistic and knew that having had two positive reactors we weren't exactly sitting pretty at all.

At this stage we had simply been going through the motions during the tests. We had been very accepting.

We hadn't been worried before the first skin test. We had been very worried when we were told we had a positive reactor, and now we were seemingly up a certain type of creek without a paddle! That's how we felt.

The poor calf looked so lost in his isolation pen. We kept going down to see him, but eventually about a week later he too went to the slaughterhouse as Carol had gone earlier.

Could it get any worse? Well, yes it could, and as it turned out a lot worse. Probably the worst it could have been.

Chapter 10

The Blood Test

The blood test came five days after the second skin test. We had known about it since Carol's autopsy had found at least one lesion.

We still hadn't gone into full-on research mode as yet. We'd been rolling with the punches, as is said in sporting circles. We were trying our best to get up again every time we got knocked down, but unbeknown to us at the time we were about to be not just knocked down, but completely knocked out.

There wasn't much else I could find out about what difference there was in having a blood test, other than that a blood test picks up reactors sooner than a skin test. I presumed that must make it more accurate than simply measuring skin with callipers. It made sense.

By now our worry level was reaching new heights. Looking back, when we wrote the first book, we had realised that we had never received any kind of support from Animal Health other than people coming out, conducting tests and leaving us again.

It wasn't as though they were some kind of agricultural support group, we knew that, but a little compassion would have helped.

Our next visitors from Animal Health were to be two girls. We weren't bothered about who came. They were to conduct the blood tests.

Nobody could have prepared us for what happened next.

It was now 7 April 2010.

We were all waiting for them to arrive that morning. We had

prepared everything diligently, following all protocol. We had set up the crush area once again at the far end of the cattle yard and, as we had done with the first skin test, we had halter-tied some of the cattle to be tested. These were the ones that we felt it best that didn't go through the crush.

Katie and Boxster were standing at one side of the crush.

We had kept them isolated from the rest of the cattle, even in the yard, because of their separate herd status.

Nectarine, the grandma of the pedigrees, was tied up at the other side of the crush pen. The other larger or older pedigrees, including Vi, who was one of our largest cows, and Vinnie, another great show bull and our stock bull who I had loved nearly as dearly as Boxy, were at the entrance to the yard which is midway between the farmhouse and the wood yard.

We had permanent hooks in the wall there. The cattle would stand on concrete and it's where we would wash them and conduct halter training in preparation for their show careers, getting them used to being led around a show ring.

We wanted Nectarine done and put away. She'd played her part in the success of our herd over the years and we looked after her as the grand old lady. We wanted to avoid anything that would cause her stress.

In preparation for the day, and because I thought it might help with a few of our cattle, I had brought home some local anaesthetic cream.

I didn't know whether it would help much but I had put it on anyway. It's the cream that is put on the backs of children's hands in hospitals. I know it sounds a little soft, but all I was trying to do was to give some form of comfort to our animals and I thought it might also make life easier for the Animal Health girls when taking the samples.

I'd brought it back mainly for Vinnie. He was a major needle phobic. He only had to see a needle and he would go berserk, and we didn't want that.

The last thing we needed at the moment was to have one of our animals lash out at someone, particularly someone from

Animal Health. I put the cream on his tail. There's a really juicy vein underneath the cattle's tails and that's what they generally use for the samples. I'd thought that by putting the cream onto the tails it wouldn't cause them as much discomfort.

As well as Vinnie I also applied the cream to Nectarine, Vi and Boxy. I'd done it all during the time we were setting up for the day whilst Dad and Melvin, one of our farmworkers, were tying up the cattle.

The Animal Health girls introduced themselves.

We changed their names for the purposes of this book, at the request of Animal Health and, in our opinion, to save the girls from never again being able to hold their heads up high, certainly in agricultural circles.

You will see why, although during that day everything seemed all sweetness and light.

We decided to call them Britney and Beyonce in the first book, so we'll stick with those. Humour us once again, but these are the only occasions we have ever been able to have a little fun at these girls' expense – and we could have come up with even worse names! Our other thoughts were Venus and Serena, because they're used to going to court!

I told Britney and Beyonce how we had set everything up and the order in which we would prefer to have the animals tested. I also told them that I had put the cream on Vinnie because I was concerned about his reaction to the needle, but that the cream would take a little time for it to take effect. I'd suggested we get to him a little later and they were okay with that.

I'd put it on the others more because I'd already put it on Vinnie and had plenty left rather than because I felt they really needed it.

Mum, Dad, Paul and I all took up our places. John and Melvin – John being another of our farmworkers – were there too.

Britney handled all of the paperwork, whilst Beyonce took the samples.

Nectarine was first, as we had suggested because of her age. She held a special place in our hearts and we just wanted her to go through this ordeal as quickly and painlessly as possible.

Beyonce took the sample from Nectarine. In true Nectarine style she gave a little moan, as she had always done whenever any needle had ever been inserted. The blood was taken easily. Beyonce passed the sample to Britney and she labelled it.

The vials used by Animal Health for the purposes of a blood test are around six millilitres. They are supposed to fill the vial and then invert it eight times. Following the inversion, the vials are then placed into a heated storage pad to keep the blood at body temperature. That was Britney's role.

Boxy was next.

We weren't to know just how significant the actions of the next few minutes were to be to our future.

At the time all I was concerned about was that he was okay with the actions of the girls.

For some reason it seemed as though he was really edgy that day. Normally he was so placid, but this was different. Looking back now I wonder just whether this could have been some kind of sign.

He was bawling out a little and looked wide-eyed.

He always seemed to pick up on any tension. It is said that most animals can read humans' body signals when they are around them and I know that I was extremely anxious that day. We all just wanted to get through the test. We were all on edge. That could have been something that affected him.

But it wasn't just that.

In the past few weeks he'd been jabbed in the neck; he'd been away from the rest of the herd completely, albeit with Katie; and at the end of the day he was a bull who wasn't able to perform because of the isolation. You couldn't blame him for feeling a little nervous and agitated. He was now back in another situation where strangers were around him and there was another needle on the way.

When I had applied the local anaesthetic cream I had used a

bandage to help it absorb. Before Beyonce inserted the needle I had removed it. Beyonce walked over to Boxy.

She didn't talk to him, didn't touch any other part of his body to reassure him. This girl didn't have any kind of veterinarian's version of a doctor's bedside manner.

Beyonce simply picked up his tail and jabbed him quickly. She had done it at arm's length. It was more of a straight arm jab that a boxer tries when testing out his opponent than a measured, controlled approach. It obviously unnerved Boxy because he bawled loudly. He started jumping about, almost dancing and getting himself into a real state.

It didn't do much for Beyonce either!

She jumped in fright. I don't know how many of these blood tests she had ever done, but at that moment she looked way out of her depth.

Everyone who has ever been around animals knows how important it is to build up their trust, and even more so when you are about to do something to them that is different to the norm. Here was a girl acting more like some kind of 19th-century fencing competitor with a needle and syringe rather than using a caring, friendly approach.

Beyonce dropped the vial!

You might think that this was the most significant moment of all, but this was just the beginning, the catalyst for a series of events that all occurred in the next few minutes.

We didn't understand the significance of all of this until much later.

Beyonce was visibly shaken by Boxy's reaction to her jab. She then shouted across the crush area to Britney to bring her another vial. Britney must have only heard Beyonce's voice rather than what she was actually saying because she came around at once, but she cannot have been able to make out what she had been saying in the commotion because she came empty-handed.

As Britney moved back to get Beyonce a fresh vial, Dad made a quip along the lines of, 'I hope you're going to be quicker than this, otherwise it's going to take us into tomorrow.' I'm not certain the girls would have thought much to his sense of humour, but the rest of us enjoyed it.

By now I had gone to Boxy's head and was trying to calm him. I wasn't managing it very successfully. He'd so clearly been shocked by the jab and he was now more nervous than ever. I'd never seen him as stressed as this before, even when he'd had his eye trouble the previous year.

I managed to cool him down a little, but I had to come away from where I was standing next to his head because if he had made a sudden movement forward I could have been trapped against the crush pen. He wasn't happy at all.

Beyonce tried again. She jabbed him and this time the blood began to enter the vial.

But Boxy wasn't settled at all. He was dancing about and Beyonce was trying to move with him, her vial once again held at arm's length.

She looked terrified, as well she might. Gentle giants like Boxster may well be gentle when they are being well treated but can cause severe harm when they are rattled.

Boxy was now way beyond that stage. He wasn't just rattled, he was being messed about and he didn't like it.

When you think of it like this: he'd been moved from the rest of the pedigrees for weeks, probably bewildered at what he had done wrong, now he'd been jabbed twice in a couple of minutes – he was not happy at all.

Beyonce lost the vacuum in the vial!

The vacuum sucks the blood from the animal and once you lose suction you cannot get any more blood into that same vial. Her problem was that the amount she had taken up to that point wasn't sufficient blood for the test.

Two vials down and she attempted to start on a third.

Boxy was by now as close to going loopy as I had seen. Dad made his way around to his head to try to calm him. He grabbed Boxy's nose and nose ring, and held him tightly up against the crush pen. This was all starting to get frightening. Boxy was still not settled, even though Dad was doing all he could to restrain and calm him.

Beyonce looked absolutely terrified. Dad could have ended up getting hurt because he was where I had been previously. Beyonce was very obviously concerned about her own health and welfare.

Boxy's full sample still needed to be collected. I thought that the way things were going he could very well also end up hurting himself.

On her third jab, again at arm's length, she managed to take another half-sample's worth of blood.

At that point she decided what she had was enough.

I think we'd all had our fill of drama by then. All I can remember thinking was, 'Thank god for that', because at least his test was over. It had been quite an ordeal.

Beyonce told us that she hadn't managed a full sample, but that she would mix the two samples she now had.

I think she realised that a fourth jab may have been catastrophic for all of us. She took off the bungs on the two sample vials, mixed them into one vial, replaced the bung and handed it to Britney. It was over.

It was those few minutes that condemned Boxy, although we weren't to find that out for a while yet.

However, it was also the action taken by Beyonce, both at that time and subsequently, that also became his saviour.

Light-heartedly, Beyonce told us not to tell anyone, but that she shouldn't have done what she had just done. She was talking about the mixing of the vials. We thought nothing of it at the time mainly because we were so glad that Boxy's test had finally been completed and he could settle down again.

Once Beyonce had moved on to Katie there was a palpable sigh of relief around the yard.

Katie was a little bit edgy when her sample was taken but nothing like Boxy had been. Her edginess probably came more from the fact that she had been alongside him whilst all the action had taken place for his sample.

And that was it for Nectarine, Boxy and Katie. They were all returned to their pens.

We were going to move on to the other larger cattle that we had tied up at the farmhouse end of the yard. That had been my earlier plan, but that group included Vinnie.

After seeing how Boxy had reacted I really didn't feel that it would be a good idea to try taking Vinnie's sample right then.

I knew that the local anaesthetic cream hadn't made the slightest bit of difference to Boxy and I felt that perhaps it might be better if we gave Vinnie a while longer with it on his tail.

I also didn't fancy another tricky vial-gathering session straight away. We all needed a break from that and to get some easy ones in if we could.

Dad was okay with leaving Vinnie, Vi and two of the other pedigree bulls tied up where they were. He was training up the two bulls for the show team, not that we had any immediate prospect of that any more.

'It won't do them any harm to stand there all day on the halter,' is how he put it, so we left them and started on with the herd in its entirety coming through the crush.

If we thought it was going to get any easier, we were very much mistaken.

Beyonce was not exactly having a good day. She had difficulty with quite a few of the cattle. I don't know whether the rest were reacting in sympathy to Boxster's experience or whether she was just fairly pathetic around animals. It seemed like both to me.

Her now seemingly increasing lack of confidence and poor animal husbandry technique had many of them nervous and dancing around.

With some of them she went into the neck to get the blood out of the jugular vein because she was finding the area underneath the tail was very tricky for her to get a sample.

The crush area became a clanging, cacophony of traumatised cattle thrashing about. The robustness of the equipment was well and truly tested that day. It was one long, excruciating day of clanging crush side gates and release gates, moans and grunts of animals going through. It was just horrible. The whole herd now sensed something was terribly wrong. This young girl had totally upset them.

A pedigree heifer came into the crush and she was going berserk. Yet again Beyonce was struggling with getting a sample. She jabbed her a couple of times. This particular heifer was one of the best in our latest crop and was in the running to make our show team. We had been considering her for training up because we thought she had great potential.

I tried to help Beyonce because she was so obviously struggling to take the heifer's sample. I held her tail. Beyonce held it too. The heifer continued to dance about manically in the crush. Then I felt a 'pop'!

Beyonce got her full sample, but when we let the heifer's tail go down you could see it was broken!

So now we had a possible show heifer with a wonky, broken tail. Great, what a morning! The herd in uproar, stress everywhere to be seen.

It was time for a break.

Mum conducted her usual, legendary hospitality – sandwiches, cakes, chocolate bars, teas, coffees, drop of whisky, normally for warmth of course, but after the morning we'd had you could easily say it was for medicinal purposes.

By way of a brief interlude and to add a light moment at this point I have to say that I remember watching Britney as we were eating. She was stick-thin and yet all she ate was Kit Kats!

I thought how life is totally unfair. I've only to look at chocolate and I put on a few pounds and this girl seemed to live on the stuff and was as slim as she was. Cow!

If I've painted Beyonce and Britney as villains so far then I should rectify things a little here.

We all felt they were nice girls when they arrived, and we chatted with them amiably at lunch. We had no axe to grind with them, not just yet.

I had been surprised at Beyonce's lack of empathy with the cattle she was about to put a needle into, but that had been all. I'd been concerned for her when Boxy had become stressed.

After lunch we made our way back to the yard. We reached the four animals that were tied up and decided they would be next.

One of these was Vinnie, who I had been worried about. Before Beyonce attempted to collect his sample, I removed the bandage from his tail. He didn't react to the bandage being taken off, or his tail being lifted. The local anaesthetic cream seemed to have worked. When Beyonce inserted the needle into his vein he made no reaction at all. He was as good as gold.

The other three tests all went well too, then we moved on to the rest of the herd that we still had to put through the crush.

It had been a horrible day all round. The weather was murky, dull, cold and miserable. We were relieved when the tests were completed and every animal had supplied a sample and was back where it should be.

We hadn't had time to worry about what the results might hold and by the end of the day we were simply exhausted.

Chapter 11

Bloody Hell! – The Results

We knew that the results wouldn't come back straight away, but we didn't know when to expect them. That's why Dad had a telephone conversation with Crispin Madavo the following day. Crispin told him that it would probably take about a week for them to come through. We were anxious, but no more anxious than we had already felt.

Crispin asked how the blood test day had gone and how the girls – Beyonce and Britney – had got on. Dad said they had been 'right enough girls' and it hadn't been a very pleasant job for them, nor any of us.

We were back on tenterhooks, waiting for the phone call that would hopefully give us some comfort from this nightmare.

When it came it offered anything but that, our nightmare was complete!

It was Mum who rang me. It had been five days since the test. All she said was, 'Can you come down here?'

Andrew and I lived a mile or so away from the farm with our son Patrick and daughter Gemma.

I was wary. Mum would have told me straight away if it had been good news. I answered her somewhat warily.

'Right. Yeah. What's the matter?'

I felt hollow when she told me. It was as though someone had knocked everything I had inside of me right out of my body.

'Well, we've got the results of the blood test. You'd better come down.'

I jumped into the car and flew round. I felt numb again. We

had been expecting the results, but expecting them and actually receiving them were two very different states of mind, as we were to find out.

As I walked through from the kitchen to the living room I could see that she was distressed.

Mum's first words were, 'It's not good. We've had six reactors.' Crispin had rung with the results.

She paused for a second, gathering herself but also trying to prepare me as she was about to deliver the worst possible news.

Her face told me before she put it into words.

'... but one of them...'

And I knew for certain. It was Boxy. I just couldn't believe it. After all we had done to keep him away from being susceptible Boxy was a positive reactor. I looked down at the numbers Mum had written down that morning. It was there in black and white. It showed his ear tag number. It was the first on the list of six.

I turned and walked out of the house.

I went straight to the field. Boxy was in his isolation pen. I stood looking at him in the field and burst into tears. I hadn't been prepared for this. No matter how much I had tried to make sure the farm had been free from disease it hadn't worked.

And this was the cruellest moment of them all.

I knew the result would mean that Boxy, our finest show animal of all time and the bull that I had built up such a special relationship with, would have to go.

I don't know how long I stayed at the fence. I just stood there. Boxy came up the field to see me and I talked to him. All I could do was cry and then cry even more. At some point whilst I was at the fence I phoned Andrew to come down to the farm. He was on his way home from work. I needed him with me but also I just needed to be there with Boxy.

Mum came out to check on me and to get me to come back in. I stayed outside a little more, cried a bit more. At that moment I just wanted to be in my own little world. I had no thoughts of planning to keep Boxy alive at the time. I had felt that was it. I kept looking at him thinking this was the end, it was now just a matter of time before he would be going to the slaughterhouse.

By the time I returned to the house Andrew had arrived. He gave me a hug and tried to reassure me that everything would be alright, but I didn't feel there was any way this could be made right.

This was how Mum felt:

'I was devastated. I felt sick, physically sick, because we'd gone into the test thinking positively. We had convinced ourselves that everything was going to be alright. Now, suddenly, with these six reactors, not just one at a time any more, the momentum was picking up. Things were getting out of control.

'The day we found out we had six reactors I wrote the numbers down, and as soon as I wrote the first number I knew it was his. I do all of the paperwork, including all of the movement records and so I was used to seeing his number but I checked anyway. I just remember saying, as soon as I saw the form … "It's Boxster".'
Anita Jackson

We had to move Katie out of the isolation pen straight away. She was put back with the rest of the pedigree herd.

The rest of that day I spent in my own little world. Looking back that's what I needed to do at the time until I had accepted what had happened. It took me until later that evening to get over the shock of it all.

That's when I started thinking positively again, gearing up for a fight.

Boxy hadn't gone yet, we'd only had the result through. I kept asking myself why he could be positive as a reactor when he hadn't been mixed with the herd. He'd passed his skin test. He'd had no lump at all. He'd had nothing to give concern. He had lived with Katie, just the two of them together. How could she pass her test and yet he hadn't?

Everything spun around in my head, but at least now I was passed the tearful stage and was moving forward with some kind of purpose.

And it wasn't just me who was gearing up for a battle either. Boxy was not just the animal I pampered and paraded around a show with, he had also been my dad's high hope for a successful 2010 show season.

This is how he reacted:

'All I said at the time was that I was going to ask for a re-test. I wanted to be sure that the test was correct, and because the girls had experienced problems getting his sample I wondered whether there was anything that could have gone wrong with it. I was prepared to pay for any re-test.'

  Ken Jackson

Going through my head at the time was the thought that Boxy had proved in the past that he had a really unusual immune system. The problem with his eyes had begun, we had found, because he was allergic to a strain of grass; he'd then become allergic to the antibiotic drops that he'd had prescribed for his eyes; when he had been injected an earlier time, not for TB, a lump twice the size of a tennis ball had come up. He'd also previously had antibiotics injections, prior to Great Yorkshire Show in 2009.

When a lump had come up to one side of his bum after the first injection we had made sure that the second injection went in the other side of his bum, so that if another lump came up he would have matching lumps either side. It worked!

All of these things gave me the feeling that his immune system wasn't quite your average everyday system. We're all different and we all have different reactions to things, perhaps his blood test fell into the same category?

I know that some people might think I was clutching at straws, trying to find anything I could to save him, that's exactly what I was doing.

I had to find something. That's when I started questioning whether the injection of bovine TB he'd had into his neck on 12

March had been held onto in his body longer than your regular animal. My reasoning was that if he was more sensitive to elements being administered into his body than other animals, perhaps that made a difference.

The six animals identified, including Boxy, were issued with a slaughter notice the following day.

We were also told that 20 animals were to be re-tested due to poor sample quality and on 14 April re-sampling took place.

Britney came back, but there was no sign of Beyonce this time. We all thought she must have had enough after her previous visit. This time they sent a chap with Britney.

Four of the six condemned animals who had tested positive through the blood test were slaughtered on 15 April. The four that went were all commercials.

The other reactor, along with Boxy, that we didn't let go at first was another of our pedigrees, a Blonde cow.

There was a simple reason – we hadn't been issued with a movement licence as she had to go to a different abattoir due to being older than the other four.

Eventually we were issued with one and we sent her, although at the time it appeared to us as though Animal Health tried to make out we were playing them up over this. We kept both the Blonde cow and Boxy!

Up until now we had asked a lot of questions, but we hadn't got tough. We hadn't challenged anything properly.

This was where we started digging our heels in. We had decided that we weren't sending Boxy to slaughter.

This wasn't just because of one girl's love of her favourite bull. Boxy was definitely that to me. He was also Hallmark Boxster, champion of champions in the show ring, and as such was worth a lot of money.

Showing cattle is about love of, and pride in, animals and breeding quality. It is also about a social activity, it is also a professional hobby, but it is also the shop window for your stock – and given the previous year's successes Boxy was now an extremely valuable animal.

He was already worth tens of thousands of pounds in a sale ring, if we had ever considered selling him, and his breeding potential, selling semen straws, was immeasurable.

No, no, no, we weren't going to give Boxy up without a fight – and we intended to fight all the way!

We refused to send him to be destroyed.

Chapter 12

We Want a Re-Test

Crispin Madavo visited us twice in April 2010.

We put our case. We were still dealing with Animal Health as though they were gods at this time, effectively doffing our cap to their officialdom, but all of this was about to change in the coming days and weeks.

This soon became us versus them and a fight to the bitter end, hopefully theirs not ours, but we were taking on a government department. We were the minnows, the underdogs. We were David to their Goliath.

We explained how we felt that Boxy's immune system perhaps being different may have had an impact on the tests.

Dad kept telling Crispin that we were prepared to pay for a re-test, but Crispin wasn't having any of it.

Crispin was playing it straight by the Animal Health rule book rather than thinking that this might be an anomaly, a case that didn't fit the regulations.

We kind of knew that people who are basically government employees were unlikely to bend, but we also felt we had a strong enough case.

All we were pinning our hopes on right then was that Animal Health would sanction a re-test and we didn't see what was so wrong with that.

Our logic had been that Animal Health had decided they needed to re-test 20 of the herd, so what difference would it have made to re-test Boxy? If at that point he'd proved to be a positive reactor we would probably have felt we had no option but to let him go to slaughter.

Crispin never bent for us once.

He told us that EU law states that any animal which has tested positive to a blood test must be slaughtered. There were absolutely no special cases. Under no circumstances was there the possibility of another test. We were done. Boxy was sentenced to death. Final.

In between our two meetings with Crispin, and unbeknown to us at the time, someone else had already begun the Animal Health campaign to ensure Boxy was destroyed come what may.

Clare Taylor was Crispin's boss and although we hadn't been aware of her until this time, it was she who became our arch enemy for the next year. We were shortly to meet her face-to-face.

When we received the content of her emails sent during this period, when we went to the High Court in 2011, it only served to back up what we had thought all along, that they, Animal Health, were never going to find a way of helping us in any way, shape or form.

The following are some of those emails.

On 19 April 2010 Clare Taylor had sent what seems to have been her first email about us, on this occasion to the veterinary and technical service team. It read:

'We have a high profile confirmed breakdown that has disclosed a gamma positive pedigree bull. The owners have refused to release the bull thus far … the lead veterinary officer is unable to find clear OM guidance, and we need a fairly prompt response for this in order to manage a challenging situation… The farmer has requested the details of gamma interferon test parameters and the levels of positive titres (that were disclosed in the bull primarily)… This may require some briefing of our lead veterinary officer if they are not clear cut.'

Clare Taylor, Regional Veterinary Lead, Animal Health (Leeds)

When we saw this email it backed up what we had felt at the time Animal Health had visited. They had known they were in difficult territory. It seemed to us that even they hadn't really known what they could and couldn't impose, otherwise why mention anything about clear OM guidance? If we had seen this email at the time it had been sent we would probably have been mildly euphoric. In northern terms it looked like we already had them on the run. This was Clare Taylor asking for help. They hadn't known what to do after all!

By way of a lesson here, titres measure the quantity of a specific antibody in the blood serum. The body, providing it has a healthy immune system, forms antibodies in response to exposure to infectants. We wanted to know what Boxy's titre level had been.

We had also asked questions about using Boxy's semen for breeding purposes.

The left hand not knowing what the right hand is doing is a phrase often used to explain away ineptitude in organisations and the various emails we saw later regarding Animal Health's thoughts were laughable, if they hadn't been about something that to us was so important.

It turned out that they, Animal Health, weren't sure whether Boxy hadn't already gone to slaughter!

This is what Jane Clark, veterinary services manager, sent to a number of people including another official – how many were getting involved here? – John Montague and Clare Taylor on 22 April 2010:

'… *Leeds are preparing a report for you but it is my understanding that the bull is either in isolation or, in fact, already slaughtered. Clare, please can you ensure that TBP receive an update to clarify the TB control measures in place.*'
Jane Clark, Veterinary Services Manager, Animal Health

And that wasn't all. On 23 April 2010, and between the times of our two meetings with Crispin, Clare Taylor sent another email, which contained the following:

'As you can see from the first email, the owner is refusing to have these animals removed. We are making every attempt to achieve compliance. The owner is very knowledgeable (she is a nurse) ... Many challenges have been raised to policy... The owner has spoken to the press, the NFU, and has talked of campaigning for the bull on a national level...'

Clare Taylor, Regional Veterinary Lead, Animal Health (Leeds)

Let's take those one at a time then. Firstly, I now appeared to have been elevated to being Boxy's owner!

Secondly, I am not a nurse although it was nice to be called knowledgeable and I had been doing all I could research-wise.

Thirdly, yes, we had started talking with various people we knew at the time in the media world.

Amongst them were Chris Berry and Angela Calvert.

Chris has written for the *Yorkshire Post* for many years. He's written farming stories in their excellent Country Week section on a Saturday since the section started, and it is he who wrote the initial book and again this one through interviewing all of us. Mum, Dad, Paul, Andrew and I have known him for years and he and Dad also performed together raising funds for charity in the Singing Farmers Concerts that ran for 13 years.

Angela has written for the *Farmers Guardian* for many years.

They are both personal friends and were a great help throughout our campaigning, along with Chris Benfield who was agricultural correspondent at the *Yorkshire Post*.

At this stage we had done nothing other than to chat with them about support and advice. The two Chrises and Angela are all very professional people who know their way around the media world. But we hadn't as yet lit the blue touch paper over our own media campaign. It wasn't far off though!

Things were warming up.

Even though we didn't see those emails until the court case we were beginning to feel as though Clare Taylor was starting to panic. We were winning small battles, not significant enough to give us too much hope at that time, but Boxy was still alive.

Crispin had approved Boxy's move to his isolation paddock.

Maybe Crispin was in trouble now? It was enlightening to read these emails later on, but it would have been great to have seen them at the time. It would probably have given us greater hope.

The day prior to Crispin coming out for his second visit in April 2010 the following email was sent around the veterinary and technical services team:

'I would question whether field isolation is the best risk reduction measure in a four-year testing area.'

John Montague, G6 Veterinary Advice, TB Programme, Animal Health

To which a reply came the next day, 28 April 2010, whilst Crispin was with us. This was circulated around Animal Health, to John Montague and others. It seemed as though everyone had now been made aware of us in their organisation.

'... Whilst field isolation is indeed less than ideal it seems that we are unable to insist on this. I presume that Leeds staff have already tried to persuade the owner to isolate the animal in a building, but will copy to Clare for comment, and to ask her to keep us, and yourselves, informed on this situation, and particularly re: the essence of any further communications involving the media and/or NFU.'

Alan Hurst, Veterinary Service Manager, Veterinary & Technical Services Team, Animal Health

Crikey! Just imagine all the effort being expended on this when a simple re-test would have sorted everything out.

Remember, we were never made aware of any of these shenanigans going on behind the scenes.

Why can't government departments copy you in with what they are saying and feeling, instead of making it an 'us and them' situation?

As Dad says, you'd think we were all supposed to work

together. We had never been asked the questions that they were asking of each other internally. And this guy Alan Hurst only seemed concerned about what might appear in the media!

We read that Clare Taylor had responded, it appeared to us, pretty quickly to the Alan Hurst email on 28 April 2010 that she had been copied in to. Within half an hour she had sent a very quick message to Crispin. It read:

'I thought the bull was in isolation indoors? I must have missed that. I'm guessing that he cannot isolate them indoors?'
Clare Taylor, Animal Health (Leeds)

Wow! How quick was that response? If we'd known about this at the time, I'm sure we would have had at the very least a wry smile. But surely this showed just how little Animal Health really cared about what was happening to us? All they appeared to care about right at this moment, and what to us they remained fixated on throughout, was getting rid of Boxy and what would happen in the media. Clare Taylor didn't even know where Boxy was!

If we had known all of this, and all of the paperwork and emails flying around about us, I'm sure our confidence in keeping Boxy alive would have skyrocketed.

Clare Taylor states in her email that she was guessing! How professional was that!

That's actually what we felt we were dealing with, the more this whole shambles went on, people who were guessing.

This lady didn't know our farm, its layout, or where Boxy even was! Crispin was another matter. It amazed me how many people were now getting involved. It was like everyone was trying to copy someone else in to their memos to cover their own backs in case they were caught out.

This wasn't about Boxy! It was about their jobs!

On 27 April, the day prior to Crispin's second visit during the month, he had sent a report to Jane Clark of the veterinary and technical services team, once again copying in another 11 officials!

Point 9 of his report read:

'Mr Jackson and his daughter are currently refusing the removal of the above two pedigree reactors. This is due to their opposition to the table valuation system (they estimate the value of the bull to be £12,000 and were offered this for him last year); concerns over the specificity of the gamma interferon test; and their request for authorisation to salvage genetic material by collecting semen from the bull. Policy and the science/reasons behind the gamma testing have been clearly explained to them. The owners are very well informed, and very attached to the bull (both in terms of affection and the genetics he holds). The owners are having ongoing conversations with the press and NFU. Several approaches have been made from the media and the NFU to Clare Taylor to answer questions and points of policy.'

Crispin Madavo, Veterinary Officer, Animal Health

Why was there a need to put into his report that we were 'well informed'? Would Animal Health put into another report that another farmer was an 'easy touch'? Reading all of this much later, we were of the opinion that they were sending out warning signals throughout the department. It looked like they, Animal Health, saw us as Public Enemy No.1.

When Crispin arrived on 28 April he had brought the print-out of Boxy's blood test result. If he had intended it to be the damning statistic that would convince us once and for all that Boxy had to go, he was very much mistaken.

The blood test results were based on a figure of anything over 0.1 being classed as a reactor. The blood test is actually referred to as the gamma interferon test (gIFN).

The tests are not 100% accurate.

We were never told what these figures meant, but we knew that whatever their rules Boxy was only the slightest touch over this mark at 0.15.

However, the Blonde cow came in with a figure of 0.275.

We could understand in layman's terms that the cow's result was a distance over their benchmark and that's why we then agreed that she should go to slaughter.

We felt that reading their literature only strengthened Boxy's case for a re-test because of how little over the mark his first had been. Sure, he was over the guideline they had recently discussed, but it was marginal. Surely it was marginal enough for them to consider a re-test?

Much later Chris Benfield (*Yorkshire Post*) asked Animal Health and the Veterinary Laboratories Agency to answer the questions which we had felt had gone unanswered.

Their answer to what happened with Boxy's first blood test and whether they accepted Boxster had given a false positive was reported this way:

'It's difficult to say exactly what happened in this case. Most cattle would give the same results consistently over time. However, there are a number of factors that can lead to different test results at different times, including: no diagnostic test being 100% accurate; the time elapsed between tests; and the complex nature of animals' immune responses to the TB bacteria, which are not static but evolve over time.'

Yorkshire Post – 12 September 2011

Their words were exactly what we had been telling Crispin. Boxy was one such animal whose immune system, clearly demonstrated by what we had said over his reactions to other events, had a complex nature.

If Animal Health were prepared to put all of this into writing 18 months later then why couldn't they listen to us and act on what we had said in April 2010?

In trying to find a way to make the re-test happen we had suggested that we would pay, whatever the price.

Nothing was working. Crispin was firmly of the opinion that Boxy had to go. And we were now determined that he wasn't going.

At the very least we were committed to not letting him go until he'd had another test. There was no middle ground. Neither of Crispin's visits had made any difference to our position, nor his. We were at a stand-off.

And that's when everything started getting heavy.

Funnily enough it started getting heavy at Animal Health first, although of course we only knew this later when all of their emails and correspondence were in the hands of our solicitors.

I don't think Crispin had been very happy with Clare Taylor's earlier email. I think he was hurt by an implication that he hadn't told her everything.

We felt his reply to her early in the morning of 29 April 2010 was curt, but it also contained something that was news to us.

Remember Crispin had been with us the day previously. We thought he must have felt cheated in some way, but so did we when we read this email:

'The bull was already in a field isolation (recently formally approved by me for epidemiological separation to facilitate the possibility of earlier lifting of TB2 restrictions than the rest of the herd – he is used for showing) when he tested positive to the gamma test. He has not been moved from this unit.

'I visited the Jacksons yesterday to discuss/explain gamma results and the outcome of their requests for permission to use previously collected embryos and collect semen.

'… following my explanation the gamma results were accepted. They have now agreed to release the bull for slaughter. Mr Jackson will deliver him to the abattoir … for slaughter on either Tuesday or Thursday next week. I expect to get confirmation from Mr Jackson sometime today. They continue to be unhappy about the table valuation though, and I am not sure whether or not they will pursue this matter further.'

Crispin Madavo, *Animal Health (Leeds)*

What the hell was Crispin up to here?

We never, and I mean never, agreed to release Boxy for slaughter at any stage. We had agreed that the cow should go, but why had he reported that we had agreed to let Boxy go? It didn't make sense.

Once again, we only knew about this report and these emails when we went to the High Court the following year.

But back in April 2010, even without the knowledge of these emails, we now knew that we were going to get nowhere with DEFRA and Animal Health, so it was time to mobilise our own support and strengthen our case further.

At this stage all we still wanted was for Boxster to be tested again. Given his unusual immune system, which we felt we had identified well enough, and his closeness to the gIFN cusp of positive/negative, we felt this was not out of the question.

Animal Health's view was, of course, quite contrary.

It turned out that our movements elsewhere and conversations with others were also now being monitored by Animal Health officials.

The following email was sent to Ricardo De La Rua-Domenech, a DEFRA veterinary advisor copying in several others, from Shelley Rhodes, one of their gIFN test consultants, on 30 April 2010:

'I have just heard via Martin that the owners of these animals have apparently contacted Jacky at VLA TB diagnostic section to enquire about a private IFN gamma test and have been told this is not an option. We thought you should know.'

Dr. Shelley Rhodes, gIFN Test Consultant, VLA Labs, Animal Health

We were contacting anyone we could. We had already told Crispin we would pay for any test. We were now contacting any laboratory to see whether they would undertake the test for us.

Word was getting around. We were at the very least causing them some form of irritation.

The tone of the next email, also sent on 30 April 2010, in response to Shelley Rhodes, from Ricardo De La Rua-Domenech, exemplified what we felt was the shadowy nature of the organisation. And we were also stunned by its content:

'Thanks Shelley, for the tip-off, but this is quite odd as Clare Taylor advised only yesterday that Mr Jackson and his daughter had finally agreed on Wednesday to release the gamma interferon reactor bull (and presumably also the cow) for slaughter. Perhaps the direct approach to VLA by the Jacksons took place before that? Or maybe the owners have changed their minds in the last two days?'

Ricardo De La Rua-Domenech, Veterinary Adviser, DEFRA

No matter where we turned it appeared that doors were now well and truly being slammed in our faces – and it felt as though we could not trust anyone.

We had not given Crispin any indication that we were going to allow anything to happen to Boxy.

But hold on here. On the same day – 30 April – yet another email was sent within the walls of the Animal Health department. This time it was the veterinary services manager Alan Hurst getting in on the act again.

His tone also showed just how little this government department empathised with farmers.

Work together? There's no chance of that ever happening when emails like this are flying around:

'This felt from the start like one of those cases in which we might encounter difficulties if the owners were obtaining information from multiple sources.'

Alan Hurst, Veterinary Services Manager, Animal Health

Charming! It tells you everything about what we felt doesn't it? Us versus them.

Chapter 13

The Meeting at
Selby Livestock Market

It was time for the Jackson media push to get under way.

We contacted the *Yorkshire Post*, *Farmers Guardian*, the NFU and basically anyone else who we thought could help. We had also commissioned a local valuer to estimate Boxster's worth.

We were never about to sell him, but we needed to know for our media story.

As a result of our valuer letting Animal Health know Boxster's true market value, another email was sent from Clare Taylor on 18 May 2010 to six of her colleagues:

'As you may know, we have a pedigree bull in Yorkshire that is a gamma interferon reactor. The owners (K & AC Jackson & Son) are refusing to release the animal for slaughter. We are obviously working very hard to persuade the farmer in region, and I have been speaking to the NFU and Yorkshire Post *again today on the very subject. We have just received a letter from Mr Richard Dixon, valuer for WM Sykes & Son. He has obviously been commissioned by Mr Jackson to value the bull in question. The value has been estimated at £20,000 (compared to £2,681 approx. table valuation). The main reason I am bringing it to your attention is that he has copied this to his MP (Mr Nigel Adams) and hence this question may be raised at a higher level.'*

Clare Taylor, Regional Veterinary Lead, Animal Health (Leeds)

We knew that we needed to do something because we couldn't just stay entrenched in our position. Animal Health weren't going to give up theirs. We knew that would never happen as Clare Taylor's email demonstrates. And we weren't going to be able to find anyone to test him independently, that was another door permanently slammed in our faces.

The independent laboratories gave us the impression that if they were seen to be working against DEFRA and Animal Health it wouldn't be in their best interests in the long term. We could understand that.

On 25 May 2010 we sent a letter to HRH The Prince of Wales outlining our position and seeking his support. We copied in the Secretary of State, Caroline Spelman MP; Minister of Agriculture, James Paice MP; Richard Benyon MP; Lord Henley; Nigel Adams MP; and Dominic Littlewood. We were trying desperately to leave no stone unturned.

We decided that we would try to get farmers on our side, to muster greater support. We started up a petition to get Boxy re-tested. Selby Livestock Market, where we sell stock regularly, got behind us immediately. Most of the farmers at the mart were already aware of what was going on, but the auctioneers and staff at Selby now swung into action to help.

I spoke with Richard Ellison, who at the time was our regional manager of the NFU (National Farmers Union) in the North East. We talked of a way in which we might be able to organise a meeting to let farmers in our area know more about bovine TB.

Everyone knows that bovine TB exists, but because the main concentration of the disease was at that time located in the south-west of England there were not many farmers in Yorkshire and the North East who understood it and its implications.

My plan was that the meeting would get across to other farmers what we were going through, as well as telling them more about the disease. They would be able to ask their own questions and learn how to protect themselves.

Animal Health, the NFU and local veterinary practices

would all be on hand as well as, hopefully, quite a few farmers.

I was hoping that during the meeting the questions I needed answering could be answered. The additional benefit would be that we would have a lot of back-up from the other local farmers who would attend.

What we were preparing wasn't quite an ambush of Animal Health.

Who were we trying to kid?

We would have loved it to be that way, but not because we particularly wanted to rub anyone's nose in it. We just wanted some way of getting Boxy re-tested. It was all part of a plan.

Selby Livestock Market offered their canteen as the venue for our meeting. There were a number of NFU representatives, including both Richard Ellison and Catherine McLaughlin who is an expert on veterinary matters. She is extremely knowledgeable about bovine TB.

Clare Taylor was to be the main speaker. The meeting date was set for 3 June 2010. I couldn't wait!

We had aimed the start of the meeting for three o'clock, as that was just a short while after the Mart normally finished selling on a Wednesday. They finished around one o'clock that day, a little earlier than we had imagined, but there was still a good turn-out of local farmers and supporters despite having to wait. They were behind us all the way.

Alan Hall was there. Alan sadly passed away suddenly whilst the first book was being written in February 2012. It was a shock to us all and we dedicated that book to him. He was a well-known and well-loved Blondes showman and we showed our cattle alongside each other throughout the summer seasons.

He had come down from his farm at Brafferton, near Darlington. We were chatting just outside the Mart. It was general stuff and I was out there because I wanted to be the first to greet Clare Taylor.

I wanted to be on the front foot from the start. I was up for this.

What I hadn't anticipated had been the realisation that

we already had the solution to Boxy's fate – and it came just moments before Clare Taylor arrived! It couldn't have been better timing!

Alan and I were talking through what had happened the day of the blood test. It was the first time we had seen him since our problems had begun.

I'd said how horrible it had been the day we had been told about Boxy and I told him that Beyonce and Britney had trouble with the samples. So far as I was concerned all I was doing was just relaying the events of the day, but Alan picked up on the mixing of Boxy's samples.

Alan said: 'They did what? That can't be right.'

And as soon as he had said it the penny dropped. We actually had them!

Why hadn't I thought about that? Especially coming from my background. The vials are sterile containers. They shouldn't be exposed to the air, or anything else, such as another sample. That's why they are vacuum containers. You don't open them until you are in a sterile environment.

Gotcha!

I couldn't believe I hadn't thought about it, but as soon as Alan questioned what had happened it gave me one massive dose of adrenaline. For me this meeting was no longer about clinging to some vain hope. This was the real deal.

We had them! I just knew it. There was no way they could wriggle out of it. They had mixed the vials. We had seen them. No wonder Beyonce had asked us not to mention mixing them. No wonder she didn't come back.

Boxy's test had to be null and void! They would have to conduct another test now, as we had wanted all along.

After weeks of hitting our heads against a brick wall we finally had not just a hope, but an absolute cast-iron case.

Jonathan, our vet from Bishopton Vets in Ripon, was at the meeting. Clare Taylor hadn't arrived yet, but everybody else was there. I was no longer as bothered about that initial greeting. I had a greeting that would hopefully shock her as much as we had been shocked before.

I told Jonathan about the botched blood test. The mixed vials. He looked stunned. I don't think he could believe what Beyonce and Britney had done.

I was now really excited about the meeting.

When Clare Taylor arrived and we'd exchanged pleasantries she said that she was quite prepared to discuss our issue, but that she didn't want to do it in the meeting. She told me she was happy to meet with Mum, Dad and myself afterwards.

I think she must have felt this had all the hallmarks of a set-up. She was so right on that score – and now we had her here and suddenly we had a watertight case. I was sure of it.

The meeting started and when questions came her way, I thought her answers were unclear. Dad and I asked a few questions along with other farmers. We tried to make them general questions about bovine TB and testing procedure but anyone could tell that they were related to our case.

Clare Taylor received a considerable amount of flak, which to my mind, she didn't appear to handle well.

When the larger meeting concluded, a smaller gathering took place, but it certainly wasn't just myself, Mum, Dad and Clare Taylor. It also included Alan Hall; a friend of ours with massive legal experience, who we will call Vera Gesty here; Jonathan, our vet; Brian Bartle, of Selby Livestock Market; and a number of NFU and Animal Health representatives, including Richard and Catherine from the NFU.

We spoke about Boxy's sensitive immune system. Jonathan backed us up. We talked about test accuracy.

Clare Taylor kept repeating 'policy'. Whatever question we asked, whatever possibility we came up with, her answer was 'we have to adhere to policy'.

As I'd suspected, we were getting nowhere. But I'd had my ace firmly up my sleeve during that afternoon, ever since Alan had made me think about the validity of Boxy's test.

It was time to play the card, to see how she reacted. Clare Taylor had been unyielding. She didn't appear to us as though she was going to give us a chance.

I'd held off from mentioning the mixing of vials throughout the earlier meeting, but the fact that she was now ramming 'policy' down our throat angered me so much. The ace was about to be played.

I said: 'But you don't always stick to policy do you?'

She can't have been ready for this. I suppose no-one likes a direct challenge that implies that what they have just been saying is incorrect.

She asked what I meant. I told her that when her two technicians – Beyonce and Britney – had come out they hadn't stuck to policy when they had taken Boxy's sample. She didn't seem to have any idea of what I was talking about.

It appeared obvious that back at the Animal Health ranch this method of mixing two samples cannot have been something the girls had mentioned.

Crispin, who was also at the meeting, jumped in at this point, and said it was the first he'd heard of this.

He asked, rather accusingly I thought, why we hadn't mentioned this previously. We would have done right at the start of asking for a re-test if we'd recognised what Alan had told me.

We were making waves! Maybe, just maybe, the tide was turning.

Clare Taylor appeared in no mood to stick around after this revelation. I noticed a look which seemed directed at Crispin. I don't think she was impressed with the sudden turn of events.

To my mind she wanted to be out of those doors faster than ever. She told us that she would investigate the matter. And she was gone.

I felt this must have been her worst nightmare. She had presumably been aware that she was coming into what could have been a lion's den given the circumstances. If she had thought that a slide presentation, answering a few questions and mentioning protocol, procedure and policy ad infinitum would suffice, perhaps afterwards she may have regretted it. And then we'd hit her with this!

I sincerely hoped we had ruined her night.

Catherine McLaughlin of the NFU took me to one side as we were getting ready to leave the Mart.

She believed we had something. She said that she was sure Animal Health policy stated that samples shouldn't be mixed in the field (by that she meant anywhere but a laboratory) and that she would email Clare Taylor and ask what her policy was for taking a blood sample.

Yesss! Result!

This was light at the end of our tunnel. The NFU seemed to be on our case in the right way and Clare Taylor had seemed not just wrong-footed but out of her depth.

We weren't about to leap up and down with joy just yet, but suddenly things were starting to look a whole lot better. I felt that at the very least Boxy would now receive a re-test. What else could they do?

The more I thought about what the girls had done and how wrong it had been, the more I was convinced Boxy's blood could have been contaminated.

I thought about what would have happened if such a thing took place at the hospital. The staff there would never mix samples to get one full vial. It would be a disciplinary matter. Results of a test would be quashed and a new sample provided.

I'd not thought of it at the time when Beyonce was collecting the blood because I was so wound up about what was happening. I had been more concerned that Boxy was thrashing about. She had been a girl who had been terrified of him. Both Boxy and Beyonce could have been injured.

All I had wanted was for the sample to be complete and although I had seen what Beyonce had done, the magnitude of it hadn't clicked.

We were in high spirits following the meeting. It had given us all the kind of lift we needed.

We did the Jackson thing and went to the pub!

Chapter 14

What the Girls Said

We were to find out just how much Clare Taylor had enjoyed her day at Selby Livestock Market café when we read her email at the time of the court case, which she sent direct to Alan Hurst and Jose Bis, as well as copying in various other colleagues at Animal Health the following day in June, 2010. It read:

*'I attended a NFU meeting yesterday, which was somewhat 'hijacked' by the issue of Mr Jackson's pedigree gamma interferon bull. The family and their supporters attended, with members of the press (*Farmers Guardian, Yorkshire Post *etc) that I can only assume they invited. It was a challenging meeting. We had a brief meeting with them afterwards.*

'Their issues (hence demand for a re-test) are: They believe human error could be significant (over and above QU process). They do not agree with the policy that discretion and/or re-test cannot be applied, and do not understand or agree with the reasons. They wish to challenge FFG policy directly. A new accusation was that two blood tubes taken from the bull were mixed. This came from totally out of the blue which they acknowledge but say that they didn't want to get anyone into trouble.

'I have answered this in the attached letter. Needless to say we, their OV (who is very helpful) and the NFU have been very active in explaining the wider issues, legislation and policy. At the moment though, we have somewhat of an impasse as the Jacksons will not accept the decision.

'... please expect an approach from NFU to policy for confirmation

*of their position as they have promised the Jacksons they will do so.
I explained to the Jacksons that I could not give them a direct policy
contact (which they are keenly seeking) hence this is the route they
will be taking.'*

Clare Taylor, Regional Veterinary Lead, Animal Health

She went on to mention a letter she was drafting to us, with
absolutely no intention of backing down. There never was an
attempt at any stage to say 'why don't we just have another blood
test?' All of these man-hours in Animal Health that were being
lost on this case when it could have been resolved so easily. She
also asked for a letter from DEFRA over TB policy.

Did it never occur to her that a re-test would have saved
their time, energy and a hijack in Selby Mart!

The next morning, having received an email from Helen
Ebden in the TB Communications Unit, Clare Taylor replied
with a line: 'It appears from the meeting on Wednesday (Selby
Livestock Market) that they are receiving advice from parties
who are not supportive or understanding of our position.'

Oh really? She'd worked that out all by herself?

The letter that Clare Taylor sent us, dated 4 June 2010,
contained the most frustrating reading of all. Paragraph 6 read:

*'I have investigated your allegations of 'mixing blood tubes' taking
place when Hallmark Boxster was sampled for gamma interferon
blood testing. The technicians clearly remember sampling the bull,
the circumstances, order of sampling, and location. This is supported
by their submission paperwork. They are both certain that one
blood tube only was taken from Hallmark Boxster. They do recall
the conversation that was had with you however, and that they did
admittedly mix tubes (only from the same animal) when some of
the young stock were sampled. On speaking to the VLA, the issue of
mixing is not one of procedure or methodology, but to reduce the risk
of contamination. They even carry this out in laboratory themselves.
No such contamination was identified at the laboratory during their
validation procedure. In view of all the above therefore, it is not*

possible to allow any further TB testing of the animal in question as requested.'

Clare Taylor, Regional Veterinary Lead, Animal Health

In addition, as a further kick in the teeth, we were issued with a slaughter notice for Boxy.

How could they say they hadn't mixed his samples when we had seen it in front of our very eyes? If Beyonce and Britney were not lying, as Clare Taylor was saying, then I can only conclude she must have thought we were.

Catherine McLaughlin had come back to me to let me know that blood samples should not be mixed in the field due to contamination issues. The NFU was with us. But now it appeared Clare Taylor was saying that none of that mattered.

It appeared we were close to the end once again. They were going to get their own way.

We'd thought 'Bingo!' when the mixing of samples had come up, but this letter really knocked the stuffing out of us. Remember we hadn't been privy to any of their internal emails which you have just read at this time.

All we'd had were letters like this and visits from Crispin.

Crispin came back out to see us. Clare Taylor's 'henchman' was how we now saw him. I asked whether he would mind me recording our meeting. He asked why and I explained that it was an emotional day for us. I wanted to be sure everything was documented.

We really were that close to giving up.

The girls' version of events hadn't matched with ours, but we couldn't prove it. We went around in circles. After he left, we were all in despair.

I sat on the beanbag in the living room crying, tears streaming down my face.

'We all felt worn out and shattered after Crispin's visits. He wasn't taking any notice of what we were saying. Kate and I both cried. It was out of frustration and we were absolutely broken. I couldn't

believe that nobody would believe us, or how they were treating us. Naively when you're telling the truth you think everyone will believe what you say, but either they didn't believe us or they didn't want to believe us.

'Nothing else as important as this had ever mattered in the same way. It looked like we had no choice but to let Boxster go. I don't actually cry very much and I certainly try not to cry in front of anyone, including family. I'm the mother. I'm supposed to support and be strong for everyone. Paul was the strong one this time. He's always the voice of reason and isn't as emotionally attached to the animals, but he could see what it was doing to Ken, Kate and me. He said he would support whatever we would do.

'That's also when Ken said, "They aren't bloody well doing this to us".'
Anita Jackson

'That's when I got mad. I could see what it was doing to us all. My family was getting upset. It's then that I really made the decision that they (Animal Health) were not going to tell us what to do. I'd stand by the gate with a shotgun to stop them from coming onto the farm to collect Boxster if I had to. They weren't having him. If they'd agreed to the re-test and he'd then been found to be a positive reactor I would have had to let him go, but not with the attitude that Crispin had shown. We're all supposed to work together. That's what we're always told.'
Ken Jackson

Through all of what we went through, Dad was always the one who made the final decision. He has always gone on his gut instinct. He listened to Animal Health's logic, their explanations, and he knew what he felt.

We knew that DEFRA was this big organisation that nobody dared say much against. We'd also received the impression from vets that if they took up against Animal Health or DEFRA they might in some way fear reprisals. Inside the Animal Health organisation, it seemed they dared not have one single case that contravened the norm. We were now that one case.

We were now definitely going to take them on.

Of course, in true Jackson style, we decided this whilst having a tot or two or three of Famous Grouse whisky! Well you've got to keep your strength up!

Chapter 15

Animal Health Get Tough

Animal Health visited again in June 2010, once again to conduct skin tests across the whole of the herd, all except Boxy. All tests came back negative. We'd had no reactors.

DEFRA sent a letter dated 11 June 2010, following our letter that we had copied to James Paice MP. It was sent from Stephen Brundle in DEFRA's Customer Contact Unit.

On 12 June, just over a week since Clare Taylor had sent her letter, backing up what Beyonce and Britney had told her, we wrote a letter to Mr Nigel Gibbens, DEFRA's Chief Veterinary Officer.

We stated that we were not happy with Animal Health's response. We felt they had breached policy and protocol. Our letter included the following excerpts:

'... *we strongly believe that there was a failure to carry out the diagnostic test properly ... Ms Taylor states, "I have investigated your allegations of 'mixing blood samples' taking place when Hallmark Boxster was sampled for gamma interferon blood testing... They (the technicians) are both certain that one blood test only was taken from Boxster..."*'

Nigel Gibbens' response came in a letter dated 1 July 2010. He replied that it was their policy to re-test when the procedure had been breached, but in our case this had not happened. He was backing the stories that had been told by Beyonce and Britney.

Here's his letter:

'Dear Mr Jackson,

'Thank you for your letter dated 12 June 2010, further to your previous letters to officials and Ministers, regarding your British Blonde bull 'Hallmark Boxster'. I have followed up the concerns you raised with colleagues in Animal Health.

'You quite rightly point out that our policy is to agree a retest if there is evidence that the original test had not been carried out properly. However, I have been assured that Animal Health carefully investigated your suggestion that the Gamma Interferon test (on one of your animals) was not carried out correctly and found no evidence that this was the case. As you mentioned, there were two Animal Health technicians present on the day. They have both reported that only one blood tube was taken from Hallmark Boxster, although they did mix tubes (from the same animal) when sampling some of the young stock and discussed this with you. However, even if the contents of two part-filled tubes had been combined into one this would have no impact on the results of the test carried out at the Veterinary Laboratories Agency, provided the sample had passed the quality controls, which it did. Blood samples cannot be contaminated with M.bovis (the bacterium that causes bovine TB) from the environment, as the test is not looking for the bacterium itself.

'I understand that Animal Health sent the NFU the procedural guidance for taking blood samples for the Gamma Interferon test some time ago.

'I realise that the contents of this letter will disappoint you but would emphasise that it is precisely because TB is such a significant and worrying problem that – to minimise the risk of disease spread – control policies must be applied dispassionately and with consistency and rigour. In the light of the above I would urge you to release your reactor bull for slaughter.'

Nigel Gibbens, Chief Veterinary Officer, DEFRA

It was around this time that we realised we would be best organising some form of legal representation.

Things were about to get heavy and we needed to know what we should do when Animal Health finally insisted on Boxster going to slaughter, which they pretty much had done here.

Richard Ellison had put us on to Jacksons Solicitors.

Would you believe it! Highly appropriate you might think, but they were not in any way a family connection.

The agricultural show season was by now well under way. We couldn't exhibit our animals because of the restrictions and we didn't attend too many.

We went to the Great Yorkshire Show, the show we all love, without our cattle for the first time in years.

We went on the Tuesday morning and as I walked into the cattle lines one of the commercial cattle handlers, Ann, came to me. She walked up, put her arms around me and told me she was so sorry about what we were going through.

I burst into tears. I'd been alright up until that point. I found it heartbreaking watching the activity in the show ring. All I could think was that I should have been in there with Boxy.

Becci Seels took the breed champion with her British Blonde heifer Cadbury.

Becci and I had grown up showing and competing against each other. We had never been best friends, but we'd had a mutual respect and liked each other.

I'd had an accident at the Great Yorkshire Show a few years previously and Becci had got hold of me and sorted me out.

I was asked to present Becci with her trophy, which was a lovely idea in one respect, but all I could think was that I hadn't had the chance to win. I wasn't jealous. If I'd been in the show ring and Becci had won, I would have thought fair's fair, but at that moment it didn't feel at all that way. Becci told me she was sorry that I hadn't been able to compete.

Little did we all know then that this would be Becci's last Great Yorkshire Show. She died of cancer the following March. That certainly put a lot of things into perspective.

What we found out at the Great Yorkshire Show was just how much public support was behind us. It was very heartening, especially with what was to come!

Animal Health's next move was to send in Andy Foxcroft.

He's Animal Health's Field Services Director for England, leading an 800-strong team of veterinary surgeons.

Were we meant to go 'Wow'? Or were we meant to feel under greater pressure because they were now sending in their big hitters? Either way we were getting beyond the point of caring who visited, it was always going to be the same result.

That doesn't mean we had given up hope, it was just that we were now wary of them. Their response so far hadn't done anything to make us think that our words were falling on anything other than deaf ears.

We had been told that Andy Foxcroft and Linda Evans, who visited with him on 16 July 2010, were very knowledgeable people about bovine TB. Linda Evans was a veterinary service manager with Animal Health in the South West.

Maybe this would be a better meeting.

I'd been doing more digging, preparing our case again.

I'd looked at the mixing of samples and I'd put together notes about Boxy, his location at the time of the blood samples, his immune system history. It also formed a log of events.

It was only a couple of pages, but it set an agenda. Hopefully it would keep us on track and give them something to take away.

We held the meeting in a barn that we use for social events. There's a long table in there and Mum had put on yet another of her wonderful spreads of cakes and buns. We might not have liked Animal Health very much, but we were still convivial.

Richard Ellison and Catherine McLaughlin attended. Andy Foxcroft and Linda Evans seemed to be listening intently.

Andy Foxcroft talked again about setting a precedent by having a re-test and that the trouble was that protocol stated that any animal testing positive had to be slaughtered.

We reiterated our concerns of the validity of the test because of the mixing of samples.

We were back to going around in circles again, but there seemed a positive side. Andy Foxcroft gave us the impression that he was going to see whether he could find a way to allow a re-test.

Our hearts rose. He had given us hope.

He left promising that he would ring in a few days. A week later he rang to say he was still working on it.

The following week he called to say that he couldn't do anything. There was a letter in the post to us. We had once again been given false hope.

When the letter came it didn't arrive on its own. With it came another letter from Clare Taylor.

The contents were yet another hammer blow. It stated the date and time they were coming to collect Boxster.

Animal Health had set the date for collection as 12 August 2010 at 11am. It was an ultimatum.

We would have to comply with removal on that date or he would be removed by force. It seemed to us, from the tone of her letter, that she was enjoying it. This is how she put it:

'As you know we have investigated your concerns and are satisfied that the samples were taken correctly and that the test is valid. You will appreciate that slaughter must now be arranged without further delay in order to maintain our efforts to control the spread of TB within cattle.

'I have arranged for collection on Thursday 12 August 2010 at 11am. The reactor will be transported to a slaughterhouse, slaughtered immediately, and a post mortem examination carried out. Animal Health officers will attend along with Trading Standards. I would ask for your assistance in loading the reactor to ensure that this is as safe and stress free for him as possible, please.

'If you would prefer a date and time prior to the above, we will make arrangements (but I will need at least three working days' notice). Also, if you would prefer to transport him yourself, please contact us as soon as possible to allow us to co-ordinate this.

'Please be aware that you also need to attend in order to present the passport and Food Chain information. Failure to present a valid passport may result in the valuation becoming invalid.'

Clare Taylor, Regional Veterinary Lead, Animal Health

It was time for our legal representation!

Chapter 16

Let's Get the Legal Eagles On It!

Boxster now had days left to live.

Our solicitors wrote to DEFRA on 6 August 2010 setting out our case and asking for an immediate response.

Here are the main points they made on our behalf. If DEFRA and Animal Health thought we were simply going to roll over, this showed we were most certainly not!

I would have loved to have seen their faces when this landed on them. They weren't taking Boxy, no matter what they thought! Here are the main points from Jonathan Fletcher's letter, our solicitor. He got straight to the point!

'According to our client the technicians attempted to take blood on three occasions, partially filling two vacutainers and mixed them in the field contrary to paragraph 8.4 of the manual, commenting to our client at the time 'you haven't seen me do this'.

'It appears that Animal Health is not so confident of the results of its investigation as was represented to you to allow you to respond to our client on 1 July. At the meeting with our client on 16 July 2010 Mr Andy Foxcroft, Animal Health Director England, was prepared to concede that Animal Health recognise that the blood tests did not happen 'as per the Operations Manual' but commented that 'that's just reality'. Further Mr Foxcroft confirmed that he '100% believed' our client's version of events.

'It appears to be conceded therefore, that the Animal Health

technicians acted contrary to their own procedures and that as a result it is conceded that their actions might lead to contamination problems.

'We consider this to be a material failure to follow protocol, for which you are unable to put forward any proper reason. Indeed not only has no proper reason been put forward to explain the failure to follow protocol there are clear indicators that rather than seek to explain their conduct the Animal Health technicians instead have misrepresented the position and sought to conceal their breach of protocol at least during the course of Animal Health's investigation into the matter, the results of which were recounted to you on 1 July.

'Despite protestations with respect to the immateriality of following procedure set out in the Operations Manual by you and Animal Health, we assert on behalf of our client that this is powerful supporting evidence of irrationality in the decision made to refuse our client's request for a re-test. It is a flawed argument to assert immateriality of the failure to follow procedure in circumstances where you, the decision maker, fail to follow guidance which you have imposed upon yourself, presumably on the basis that there is good reason to do so.

'Accordingly we consider that a judge is likely, on judicial review, to overturn the decision of Animal Health not to re-test Boxster and formally request on our client's behalf that you immediately advise whether or not you are willing to agree to do so without the need for time consuming and undoubtedly costly court proceedings.

'Given the timescales involved (Boxster is due to be collected for slaughter on Thursday 12 August 2010) we have advised our client that, in the absence of your agreement, urgent application for interim injunction, pending the determination of our client's claim for judicial review, to prevent the destruction of Boxster is necessary. Unless we hear from you by 4pm Monday 9 August 2010 that you consent to re-testing we will be forced to place the matter into court.

'Alternately, if you require a longer period to reconsider the matter, we should be grateful for confirmation by 4pm on Monday 9 August that you are prepared to grant a 'stay' so far as the collection of Boxster is concerned, which might allow the parties to conclude this matter *without recourse to court proceedings, in the spirit of the pre-action protocol for judicial review, terminable on five days' notice whilst accepting that our client would still be required to commence his court proceedings, whether or not a decision or agreement had been reached, within three months of the Notice of Intended Slaughter, being the date of the disputed decision.*

'Our client would in those circumstances, of course, be agreeable to keeping Boxster isolated in accordance with his present restrictions.

'We look forward to hearing from you as a matter of urgency and at the latest by 4pm on Monday 9 August 2010.'

Jonathan Fletcher, Jacksons Solicitors

This gained us our first small victory.

DEFRA extended their deadline for Boxster's slaughter by 14 days whilst they consulted their legal team. His new slaughter date was 26 August.

Chapter 17

Champion Without
Entering the Ring

August is usually a very busy month for us in the agricultural show rings throughout Yorkshire. There are so many good shows to choose from and we get to as many as we can, but not in 2010.

We were busy fighting the battle to keep Boxy alive, and at the very least we were fighting for his blood sample re-test. But amazingly, whilst all of the legal machinations and politicking were going on, Boxy managed to win a title whilst just standing alone in a field!

He was awarded the title of Best British Blonde Stock Bull in the Blonde Society's North East Club and was put forward as a contender in the national awards. It all happened during that first week of August.

We were stunned when we were told he'd won. Any other time it would have been the best possible news and it still was great to hear, but we had much bigger things occupying our mind at the time. We couldn't celebrate too hard, although we may have had anther Famous Grouse or two!

Chapter 18

Time to Injunct

The rest of August was tough.

We were back on the research side. I spoke to colleagues in the laboratories at the hospital where I worked, about their policies and procedures of blood sampling and how blood sampling works. I tried to find out more about contamination. How samples can become contaminated.

I just knew in my own mind that whatever they (DEFRA) were saying, contamination was a high possibility. Looking at it using their logic, they had proven, to some extent, that there was bovine TB on the farm.

From an environmental point of view that meant there was a risk of contamination. Beyonce had taken a blood sample from Nectarine.

She didn't change her gloves between dealing with Nectarine and Boxy, in fact she didn't change them at all until the afternoon.

To my mind that meant Beyonce had gone to Boxster wearing contaminated gloves. Beyonce had also taken the bungs off Boxy's samples with the same contaminated gloves.

Later on, and coming soon in our story, Nectarine recorded a positive test and also had to be slaughtered. Connected to the earlier contaminated gloves? I thought it might be. I was just conducting research into every possibility, every angle.

But bad news always seemed just around the corner and August was no exception. We had been happy in June when no reactors were found following a skin test.

You need two 'clear' rounds of skin tests to ensure the herd is 'clean'. We knew that even if we were in the clear the farm was still effectively quarantined because of Boxy, but it would have been a step in the right direction.

Our herd's next skin test was conducted on 10 August. This time it was a big chap who came. There was little chat.

The atmosphere between Animal Health representatives and ourselves was now frosty to say the least. We always tried to be friendly, but we had become wary.

Dad didn't even want them on the farm any more.

This big chap just shaved the cattle, jabbed them, real matter-of-fact, and went on his way. We awaited the results three days later.

That was another unhappy experience.

On 11 August 2010 we received a letter from Jonathan Fletcher of Jacksons.

He was letting us know that what we were trying to achieve had limited chance of working out as we would wish. This is how he put it:

'... *your claim has prospects of success, which fall below that which I would consider would allow me to advise you to commence Judicial Review proceedings.*

'I have rehearsed with you the cost consequences of commencing these proceedings and you are already aware of the outcome of the High Burrow case and the costs awarded against that farming business when DEFRA was successful in defeating their claim.

'You have advised me, however, that in any event you wish to proceed.

'The risk reward analysis weighs against you, bearing in mind particularly that even if you are successful the decision that you will overturn is the refusal of DEFRA to grant a re-test. There remains, therefore, the possibility that even if successful, Boxster might fail when he is re-tested for the TB virus.

'Nevertheless, I am happy to represent you in relation to this matter and will keep you advised in relation to any response from DEFRA to the letter before action.

'It is my intention to request that DEFRA agree not to insist that we injunct them to preserve the life of Boxster pending the full Judicial Review hearing. I think there is a good prospect that DEFRA will agree to that. This does mean, however, that we will be obliged to place the matter into court sooner rather than later (in any event, applications for Judicial Review only have a three-month limitation period from the date of the decision, which we are taking to be 29 July 2010 based upon Clare Taylor's letter and Notice of Intention to Slaughter).

'At this stage I should be grateful if you would consider emailing me and Nigel Kidwell, my Managing Partner, as much information as you possibly can to allow witness statements to be finalised...'

Jonathan Fletcher, Jacksons Solicitors

Jonathan also advised us that in his opinion we had only a 20% chance of success. We knew that he was trying to give us reality rather than pie-in-the-sky hopes.

He also asked for information on a number of subjects. We sent Jacksons everything we believed to be appropriate.

On 13 August 2010 Animal Health came back with their callipers. It wasn't the big chap who came back. This time it was Avril.

We'd never met Avril before, but we were immediately happier with her attitude than we had been with any other Animal Health representative for a long time. She sympathised with our situation and was apologetic that they had to come out and test. When she started using the callipers to take the results she was a lot nicer with the animals than the others had been. She talked to them. It seemed to us that she was far more experienced.

But it was also time for more bad news.

When Avril measured Nectarine, our old grandma of the herd, she told us that she was a positive. Nectarine had always had lumps.

I said, 'No, she can't be,' more out of shock and love of our grand old lady.

Avril checked again and then told us what it was an increase of, but I didn't hear the numbers. My head was in a spin.

Dad said something like, 'Oh, bloody 'ell.'

I just turned and walked away up the yard. It was another kick in the teeth and out of any other animal on the farm she was my second favourite after Boxy.

We'd had her 14 years and I just didn't want her life to end like this. Wiping away the tears I got myself back together and came back to where Avril was carrying out the results.

Avril was sympathetic, asking whether I was okay. As she was about to leave the farm I asked whether she would measure Nectarine again. She did. It was the same result.

We had also had three 'inconclusive' reactors. Inconclusive means they read bang on two millimetres. That didn't mean the animals had to go to slaughter, they would get another chance at the next skin test two months later. If they had been found to be 'inconclusive' again they would have had to go.

As we were now more concerned about speeding up the possibility of the herd being given the all-clear we let all four go.

It was another emotional time of course, with Nectarine now having to be slaughtered, but we saw no other way.

In between Avril's visit and Nectarine going to slaughter Crispin rang us once again.

He now wanted the whole herd, minus Boxy, blood testing in the next couple of days. He told us it was 'policy'. We put them off for a few weeks but that's all we could do. The reason we put them off was because we felt they seemed to be finding any excuse to attack us by now. We felt that this was some vendetta against us because of our stance on Boxy.

We felt there was an ulterior motive here. We had found out that once you have reached a certain proportion of your herd culled because of TB reactors, Animal Health can turn around and have your whole herd culled. We felt they were coming at us as many times and as quickly as they could to reach the target they needed. There's no way we could ever prove this but, given the circumstances, it's not surprising that we were becoming more suspicious of Animal Health day by day.

According to the policies we had seen, DEFRA could only insist on a blood test if they had found a lesion at post-mortem and Nectarine hadn't been slaughtered by the time of Crispin's phone call requesting the blood test. There had been no visible lesions on any of the four carcasses. That's one of the reasons why we were becoming suspicious of their intent.

We now knew there was no other way we could ensure Boxy's future than to take on DEFRA, most probably in court.

How did we know that for sure? Here's how.

DEFRA looked to have paid no attention to Jonathan's request that they should agree not to insist that we injunct them, as we received another letter from Animal Health dated 20 August 2010.

This time it hadn't been sent from Clare Taylor.

It was from Alan Wolinski, Regional Operations Director. It read pretty much the same as Clare Taylor's previous slaughter notice, except this time it read that they would be coming for Boxy on Thursday 26 August at 11am.

But that wasn't all, not by a long shot!

Also written to our solicitors on the same date, 20 August 2010, was a seven-page letter from DEFRA's legal department, their Litigation & Prosecution team.

This was starting to sound like a John Grisham novel, the heavy hitters with government backing versus the little farming family.

Their intention was presumably to frighten the living daylights out of us.

They did not accept anything that we had said. They also denied everything that we knew had been said. And surprise, surprise, they tried to turn anything we had said around. They were trying to make us look like liars.

We knew that we were on solid ground. We felt this was bully-boy-tactics time. These are the points they raised in their letter to our solicitors:

'As a preliminary point, it is noted that the decision to slaughter Boxster was made on 13 April 2010 and your clients were informed of this at the time. A copy of the TB3 Notice is attached. Your clients have consequently been aware of this decision for four months. Judicial Review proceedings must be commenced within three months of the decision and accordingly we consider that your clients are out of time to bring this challenge. In any event, we do not consider that your clients have a reasonable prospect of succeeding a Judicial Review proceedings and we set out our reasons below.

'It is not agreed that sampling was carried out in breach of Animal Health's own procedures with regard to Boxster, nor that Mr Foxcroft '100% believed' your clients' version of events. We have been provided with a document entitled 'Notes for meeting on Friday 16 July regarding Hallmark Boxster' which we understand was prepared by your clients. In that document and, as rehearsed in your letter, the honesty of the technicians taking the samples is called into question.

'DEFRA strongly denies any suggestion that the technicians have been dishonest or are unreliable in their recollection of events. If this matter proceeds to court the two technicians taking the blood samples will give evidence to the effect that:

Their recollection of events is very clear; indeed the unusual preparatory steps taken by your clients to bandage tails and apply anaesthetic to Boxster and two other animals were particularly noteworthy.

A full blood sample was taken from Boxster at the first attempt.

As stated in previous correspondence, it is accepted that due to field circumstances some procedures were not followed when samples were taken from other animals, but this simply was not the case with Boxster.

'We also observe that, although the test was performed on 7 April 2010 and numerous communications between your clients and DEFRA followed, it was not until early June that your clients first *made any mention of a concern over the way the blood samples had been collected – at a meeting with Clare Taylor at Selby.*

'*Indeed, just days after the taking of the samples, your clients passed on praise and thanks to the Animal Health veterinary officer, Crispin Madavo, for the service provided by the Animal Health technicians, which prompted Mr Madavo to email Joseph Clay (Team leader of technical field staff at Animal Health) on 12 April 2010 to the effect that he: "… would let you know that Mr Jackson expressed his appreciation of the efficiency and professionalism with which his recent gamma blood sampling was conducted by…"*

'*Further, at a subsequent meeting with Crispin Madavo on 28 April 2010, your clients agreed to release Boxster for slaughter. Given these events, the Department is surprised that your clients first raised these new allegations in early June, some two months after the samples had been taken.*

'*… Finally, it is noted that in your letter commencing this claim, your clients made it clear that they would seek an injunction to prevent the removal of Boxster for slaughter. Boxster is scheduled to be collected for slaughter on Thursday 26 August 2010. If your clients seek a further injunction we would expect you to include a copy of this letter in your application and in any event we would expect you to let us have notice of your application. We do not consider that this is a case where an application without notice is necessary.*'

DEFRA, Litigation & Prosecution Division – Paolo Lattuca – for the solicitor

If it was intended to warn us off once and for all it didn't work. Let's just take each of their assertions or, to put some of them mildly, their pathetic attempts at queering our pitch.

Out of Time? – Was that the best they could do? They knew that there were mitigating factors. Any solicitor could deal with that.

Sampling in breach of rules – it was their word against ours. Who to believe I wonder?

Andy Foxcroft didn't say he believed us 100%. So why did our recollection differ that he had said it then? Again, down to whom you believe.

Dishonest Technicians – as the real Britney would say, 'Hit me baby one more time'.

Boxster's Blood Sample – at the first attempt? Once again, it seemed purely their word against ours at this stage.

Our Supposed Delay in telling of their Bungle – When do you let someone know? Usually once it has clicked in your brain. Had we held something back for any reason? Why would we?

Praise for Beyonce & Britney – What is the problem with saying they were 'right enough girls' doing a tricky job? And at the stage where Dad was asked about the girls we hadn't recollected the incident with Boxster and how their bungle would affect us.

Agreeing to let Boxster go – Crispin just added to how we felt the girls had lied, or he simply got it wrong.

The injunction was now needed. We instructed Jacksons to contact DEFRA. They sent a letter dated 23 August 2010, three days before Boxy was due to go to slaughter. This is what was sent to DEFRA's Litigation & Prosecution Division:

'We have our client's preliminary instructions in relation to your letter of 20 August 2010 and they are to commence Judicial Review proceedings in relation to the decision to slaughter their bull, known as Boxster.

'PRELIMINARY POINT

'The point you seek to make is disingenuous. You are well aware that the decision challenged is that to refuse to re-test Boxster, such decision being communicated to our client by letter dated 29 July 2010, accompanied by Notice of Intention to Slaughter Boxster also dated 29 July 2010 signed by Clare Taylor. Our client is well within the time limit to challenge this decision and there is no merit in this point. Please confirm by return whether or not you are seriously intending to raise this argument as it will need to be dealt with as a preliminary issue in the proceedings.

'INJUNCTION

'Your letter appears to demand that our client injunct your client to prevent destruction of Boxster on 26 August 2010. Our client proposes that on the basis that it places this matter into court expeditiously and proceeds in the same manner to a full Judicial Review hearing that your client in those circumstances might agree to consent to a stay of execution of Boxster, pending determination of the full Judicial Review proceedings. Any stay of execution being on the basis that Boxster remains suitably isolated.

'If you insist on our clients seeking injunctive relief, which we consider would be contrary to the protocols and spirit within which they are made, then please confirm the position to us by return. Any injunctive proceedings would, of course, need to be on an urgent basis...'

Jonathan Fletcher, Jacksons Solicitors

We were granted the injunction by Sir Andrew Collins on 24 August 2010.

Jonathan and his team at Jacksons had acted quickly on our behalf and we were grateful for this.

We may just have brought out the bottle of whisky again at this point. Famous Grouse anyone?

Chapter 19

Waste of Time

September 2010 didn't start well.

Our second blood test of the whole herd, except Boxster, took place on the opening day of the month.

The results provided yet another hammer blow.

This time we were recorded as having five positive reactors. At post-mortem all five showed no visible signs of lesions. It felt like we were having our herd culled for no good reason.

Whilst 'no visible signs of lesions' does not mean the animal is not infected, it seems to us and other farmers that there is no real proof that your animal has been culled for the right reason.

Based upon what we had read, we had in mind that once we reached 15 positive reactors the whole herd would be culled. We were now at 13.

It felt as though everything was stacked against us.

Jacksons Solicitors told us of a scientific expert who would write a paper for us which was meant to support our case against the mixing of vials.

The report would cost us £1500. We were already at £7500 for the injunction. The costs were starting to mount, and our farm business was effectively out of action.

This is one of the reasons why big organisations beat the little guys like us, because they can afford the costs of legal representation.

Our solicitors had cautioned us that despite securing an injunction, in their opinion, we had little chance of success at Judicial Review – and on 15 September Jonathan Fletcher sent an email which pointed out that the scientific expert the solicitors had advised us of did not support our case!

Amazing! £1500 down the drain and an expert who wasn't on our side! Brilliant!

Jonathan's email contained further nails for Boxster's coffin:

'Finally, and I think crucially, DEFRA are able to point to the deteriorating health of the herd with further positive blood test results earlier this month. You wondered why DEFRA insisted on blood tests this time around, despite the absence of lesions in the reactor identified on the skin test and this is precisely the reason why; to allow them to damn the health of the herd and convince the judge that it is even more likely that the positive test result for Boxster was correct...

'... my view in relation to this matter has always been that whilst we might well secure the injunction, which we did in more positive terms than we could have hoped for, there is a real and substantial risk of losing the action as a whole. I'm afraid that there is nothing in DEFRA's response which detracts from my view and unfortunately the discovery of further reactors in the herd and the slaughter of more of your cattle makes the prospect of success all the more unlikely.'

Jonathan Fletcher, Jacksons Solicitors

Whilst we knew only too well how difficult it appeared to be to go up against DEFRA we also felt so frustrated.

We felt we had been done an injustice and that Boxy would be put to death unnecessarily.

Jonathan's email didn't help us believe that he and his team could succeed in winning a case for us, even though it was fair to say they had helped in the first instance in achieving the granting of an injunction.

Up until this time we had never had a face-to-face meeting with Jonathan or his team but now we insisted on one.

The meeting took place at their office in Stockton-on-Tees. We picked up Alan Hall from Brafferton. Vera came with us too.

I just thought they hadn't grasped the whole story and by now we were running out of time as the Judicial Review was fast approaching. We went through the events with Jacksons once again and I felt that they understood our position and were better equipped to take the case forward.

But we were soon to meet the man who would help more than anyone else!

Chapter 20

You've Got to Have Faith

Ripon Cathedral provided the catalyst for our renewed hope, although we hadn't known it at the time.

Highly appropriate you might think.

Mum and Dad had been invited to the special RABI Harvest Festival service, part of the Royal Agricultural Benevolent Institution's 150th anniversary.

The invitation had come about because of Dad being part of the group of singers called the Singing Farmers, who we mentioned earlier and who raise funds for the charity. The cathedral service was held on 10 October 2010.

One of the charity's main representatives in North Yorkshire asked Mum and Dad how they were getting on. Mum and Dad talked about their disenchantment with the solicitors we had, because of their constant opinion that we had limited chance of success.

The charity's representative mentioned a 'really great solicitor' that she'd had when she was having trouble during foot-and-mouth disease in 2001.

The day after the service at the cathedral we received the solicitor's contact details.

His name is Richard Barker. The RABI representative had already made contact with him and told him about our story.

Richard had earned a reputation as the 'voice of the agricultural community' in legal circles. She said that he was willing to talk with us. As a stroke of luck, and we felt we were due one by now, he was stopping over in York the following week.

I rang him.

When I heard his big, booming and very cultured voice (that's 'posh' up where we come from!), I immediately took him to be the type of person you could be terrified of and intimidated by. I could imagine him speaking in court as a judge. He just had that air of authority. I hadn't prepared what I was going to say, so I started to just tell him who I was and why I was ringing him.

He was charming, absolutely lovely and told me, 'I am in York soon, my dear, overnight. If you and your family would like to come over I will happily meet you at no expense to yourself.'

This was a real shot in the arm. We set a time in the early evening of 18 October, bundled everything and everyone together, including Vera, jumped in the Jeep and off we went to York.

We must have talked with him for around 3-4 hours and we went through everything. He looked at all our documentation, flicking through.

He gave us a few questions to ask Jonathan Fletcher at Jacksons.

Richard then said that he thought we had a case, and that he was prepared to help however he could.

He said that if we wanted him to work with the solicitors we had at that time it would be the best way forward.

This was on the basis that to get right up to speed in the time he now had would be very difficult. He said that once the short-term work had been done he would then be happy to take over the case if we wanted him to, but to take things one step at a time.

He also told us that he would devote his own personal time free of charge.

After all we had been through since starting out on our case, which was all centred purely on a re-test of Boxy, we couldn't believe it!

It felt amazing, superb. I wouldn't say we left our meeting with Richard in high hopes as we may have done if this meeting had been months earlier, because we were now a little battle-hardened.

'We weren't thinking this was going to be a life saver. Thank God and the RABI is what I thought later. I do have a belief but I'm not very religious and we could easily have not gone to the service at Ripon Cathedral.

'Richard sat very quietly and listened whilst Kate did most of the talking. When he said that he thought he might be able to help it was the first glimmer of hope I felt we'd had. He didn't make any false promises and appeared very down to earth.'

Anita Jackson

We were all cautious also about whether or not we would simply be engaging another firm of solicitors who would also charge us large fees. We were grateful that Richard had said he would give his time for free, but we knew that there would be others at Barker Gotelee, Richard's firm, who wouldn't come cheap and at this stage we were still with Jacksons.

Following our initial meeting with Richard, I emailed Jonathan at Jacksons solicitors on 22 October asking what the current position was and whether he had managed to file other documents into court.

I had previously mentioned two possible scientific experts Professor Paul Torgerson and Ruth Watkins whom I had been in conversation with over the past six months and who had indicated they would be prepared to provide reports to assist us.

On 29 October 2010 we were brought to our knees. His Honour Judge Martin McKenna threw out our case!

It now appeared that, regardless of the meeting we had just had with Richard only 11 days earlier, we were finished.

These were the reasons given for refusal of permission to apply for Judicial Review:

'Even if everything alleged by the owners of the animal is accepted, if the animal in question is in fact infected and the scientific evidence is that it is highly likely to be infected, then no decision of the court can cure it still less save the animal.

'Retesting is no answer since the original test conditions cannot

be replicated and there would be no way of differentiating between a true negative and a false negative and in any event there will remain an obligation to slaughter the animal.

'Moreover the precedent created by a decision to retest would be unfortunate if allegations of minor deviations from protocol could be regarded as sufficient to justify prevention of the slaughter policy of an animal which has been tested positive in a known infected herd in a test audited as valid in accordance with applicable protocols. In any event the decision under challenge is a decision to slaughter which is made on 13 April 2010 and hence this application is out of time...'

His Honour Judge Martin McKenna

So minor deviations of protocol were okay?

And why, if we had been allowed to get to this stage were we now considered out of time? It all felt so unfair.

We were utterly devastated. We were nearly at the end of the road.

Chapter 21

All Together Now

When the news came that we had been knocked back, with the case having been thrown out, we had great support from other farmers, neighbours and those who had read about what we were going through. We were receiving fabulous support from the *Yorkshire Post*.

There was talk of forming a blockade to stop Boxy being taken for slaughter along our little single track road that winds through Walden Stubbs. Everyone would bring their tractors, 4x4s, quads and trucks.

There was another thought of demonstrating outside Animal Health's offices in Leeds.

Take the country into the city, with tractors, placards, that kind of thing. These were useful thoughts for getting our spirits up but deep down the thought was that we might just be seen as militant and nothing much more.

Barker Gotelee and Jacksons then worked together as Richard had suggested.

On 2 November, Jonathan Fletcher informed Paolo Lattuca of DEFRA (Litigation & Prosecution Division) that we would be requesting a renewal of the injunction whilst we sought reconsideration by way of a hearing.

On the same day, 2 November, Paolo Lattuca replied: 'My client proposes that it not enforce the lift of the injunction and Boxy can remain on the farm until such time as the matter is resolved, thereby avoiding the need for your client to obtain a further injunction.'

We had fulfilled the short-term objective with Jacksons.

Boxster was safe again. Animal Health did not have the

authority to come to collect him. We had bought ourselves yet more time.

As soon as we had dealt with the short-term issue of making sure Animal Health wouldn't come and collect Boxy we changed solicitors.

We spoke with Dermott Thomas, of our newly appointed solicitors on 3 November and the following day we signed the paperwork instructing Barker Gotelee to take charge and work with Jacksons to overturn the refusal.

Richard Ellison of the NFU called us asking whether Richard Barker wasn't just poaching us.

What we told Richard (Ellison) was that Richard Barker hadn't approached us, that we had approached him.

Telephone calls and emails now became all part of the daily routine, as we had anticipated they should have been earlier with Jacksons.

Dermott became our main contact, with Richard Barker overseeing everything.

I talked with Dermott, whilst Dad talked with Richard.

They talked with us about everything, so that we understood where they were coming from. We were all now heavily engaged in preparation to go to court.

And even before we could win our original case we now had to appeal against the court case that was lost!

We also kept the NFU up to speed with everything.

They had supported us financially to the tune of £6,500 but said they could not support us financially any longer.

We were already way in excess of the amount they had offered and it was all about to get far more expensive. A High Court case is not something you take on lightly, either in body, mind or wallet!

Chapter 22

Christmas 2010

We wouldn't want to paint a picture here that there weren't all the normal, everyday things going on in our home life.

It wasn't as though every single thing had been kept on hold. I was still doing school runs; the wood-chip business was still running; we were still trading cattle, but only straight to the abattoir. You can't stop work on a farm.

Dad had been gradually reducing the numbers of head of cattle for a while. He was 66 at the time and had wanted to take things easier, he just hadn't planned on TB reactors as his culling method!

Dad had continued singing regularly in pubs, clubs and village halls as he had done for years.

To anyone who came to the farm there was no noticeable difference as both Mum and Dad have this way of shrugging their shoulders and getting on with life. But I could see the strain this was causing them, and I knew it was affecting me too.

I was constantly researching for anything I could find every spare minute. I was writing up statements, and by now I was also talking with our scientific expert who I had found. He was preparing a report to go towards our court case. At this stage we had no date set, but we were now confident that it would be.

Christmas came around and of course we celebrated. We are the Jacksons and we know how to party. Have I mentioned yet our fondness for whisky? I have? Surprise!

But the atmosphere around Christmas 2010 was not what it would normally have been.

We felt that we had a firm of solicitors who believed we had a stronger case, but we hadn't yet been put to the test together in court.

Paul's wood-chip business was really busy, thank God, but he was snowed under working all the hours to get the bedding out to farms and stables. He was pushing hard to get as much business as he could. The farm was now under considerable financial strain and Paul was putting every effort into keep everything going.

We had conversations about finances and Dad was talking to the bank about land he could sell if he needed to. That shows how seriously we were taking this, because we knew that costs would escalate by taking our case to the High Court.

Seeing Boxy was heartbreaking because of the conditions he was living in. It was winter and the ground was wet and churned up. He had absolutely no cover. There had been ice on the ground too, and it had snowed a little. It was cold, wet and miserable.

Some days, as he walked towards me, I could see him sinking up to his knees into the squelching mud. I'd be at the fence and he would gradually make his way across to me. It was like one of those scenes where you see the soldiers in First World War films in the trenches. I felt his eyes looking at me saying, 'What are you doing to me? Get me out of here!'

He looked broken.

It was awful to see. I kept on ringing and emailing Animal Health to ask for the specifications of any kind of shelter we could use for him to give some form of respite. Typically, we got nowhere with them. Emails bounced around, regulations were bandied about but that was all.

In the end we came up with our own plan and did something about it. We took the livestock box off our cattle wagon and placed it on the concrete hard standing at the side of the isolation pen. We then extended his fence, including small mesh to stop wildlife from getting through, then we double-fenced, including an electric fence. It was as though he was in prison but at least he now had somewhere dry to shelter and had some hard-standing area, somewhere that wasn't muddy.

Throughout the whole of Christmastime, Boxy never came out of it. He stayed on his small area of concrete and in his box. We had at least tried to help him and give him some comfort.

Strange really that one of Animal Health's roles is supposed to encompass the welfare of animals, yet to our minds they put every effort into ensuring life was as difficult as possible for Boxy. Shame on them!

Christmas is also pantomime season. Oh, yes it is!

So, it wouldn't have been the same if our villains hadn't made an appearance, would it?

And they did! Just to make our horrible year complete, with a letter dated 31 December 2010.

It seemed to us that Clare Taylor hadn't anything better to do between Christmas and New Year other than to make our lives hell. By now we were thinking that this must have been the only way she got her kicks.

She included a few 'niggles' within her letter, which was otherwise very similar to each notice for collection of Boxster that we had received previously from her and Alan Wolinski. The letter told us that arrangements had been made for collection of Boxster on Wednesday 19 January at 11am. Merry Christmas and a Happy and Prosperous New Year! Erm… no, we've added that.

So that's how we finished 2010, with a letter from DEFRA which we felt was designed to inflict as much harm to our spirit at a time of year when everyone should have feelings of good will to all. We speculated that Clare Taylor must have had a bad Christmas herself to want to give someone else a kicking.

I sincerely hoped she had!

Chapter 23

Chip off the Old Block

Boxy was certainly happier with his environment since he had his own shelter and was able to escape from the mud, but then we started getting concerned that he wasn't coming out at all.

We wanted him to get some exercise, but we could understand why he preferred to stay under cover. His paddock was an absolute mess. That's why animals are normally brought in for the winter, to give the land a rest and chance to recover. No-one could blame him for staying exactly where he was.

There were pot-holes where he had sunk into the sludge when the ground was wet and then when icy conditions came it made land dangerous for him to walk on.

That's why in early January we decided to do something about it. And that's when we had our most uplifting moment of all.

Dad went for his tractor and bucket loader. We were aiming to fill some of those holes and pack the ground. He filled the loader with wood chip and made his way toward Boxy.

As Dad extended the arm of the tractor so that the loader was over the fence he started tipping the sawdust. Boxy came out of his shelter looking very chirpy, the most lively we had seen him for months. He was full of beans and started playing in the sawdust as Dad was tipping it in. He was play-fighting in it, rolling around like a child in a ball pool.

I was killing myself with laughter and went rushing back into the house for the camcorder and shouted for Mum. Dad had the biggest grin I'd seen on his face for ages. He went for another load, but this time when he came back Boxy creased us up with laughter even more.

When he saw Dad coming back with the second load he stood exactly where Dad was going to tip it. He was right underneath the loader and we were trying to get him to move out of the way. But he wouldn't shift at all, so Dad shrugged his shoulders and tipped it over him!

Boxy loved it. That's what he'd wanted. It was as though this was finally his playtime and we couldn't feel anything but that he deserved this moment. He was also providing us with great entertainment too.

He threw himself around in what was becoming a blizzard of sawdust. He was totally covered. There was this mass of wood chip and he was under it with legs and head writhing around. It was just quite simply a lovely few minutes and great to see him with a little bit of happiness after looking so gloomy for a long while.

And the bull that lives on was still with us no matter what Animal Health had thrown our way.

Chapter 24

The Hearing

We hadn't expected Clare Taylor's letter on 31 December, especially given the instruction we had received from their litigation unit, but we dealt with it. Dermott was now fully in control of anything that involved what happened to Boxy in a legal manner and we were discussing everything with him.

We had two main issues to address before we could take DEFRA to the High Court.

The first of those was to restrain Animal Health from sending any more notices for the destruction of Boxster whilst we were engaged in our own litigation with them; the second was to gain permission to challenge DEFRA's decision to have Boxster slaughtered.

On 13 January 2011 we applied to the High Court on three matters. The first was 'an order that the defendant (DEFRA) be restrained until further notice from putting into effect any order or notice for the destruction of Hallmark Boxster'; the second was 'an order that the permission hearing be listed on 7 February 2011 or the first available date thereafter consistent with the Claimants Counsel availability'; and the third was that 'costs are reserved'.

The following day we received our first win under the new regime of Barker Gotelee and ourselves:

On 14 January 2011 Mr Justice Williams, following consideration of the documents lodged by the Claimants, granted permission of the above three points and gave DEFRA the right to respond to the application. We then submitted our supporting evidence into court.

We were on our way.

The High Court permission hearing was scheduled even more quickly than we had anticipated. We were to make our first High Court appearance on 18 January 2011.

How did we feel? Well, after months of heartache, lies, false dawns, intransigent bureaucrats, negative solicitors and outright bully-boy tactics we felt vindicated. We were going to have our opportunity to state our case and prove that Boxy should be re-tested.

That's all we had wanted right at the start of all of this and it was still the case now.

This appearance was only to determine one thing – whether we would get the chance to state our case in a full Judicial Review. It wasn't the review itself. But it was the one and only remaining hurdle for us to jump beforehand.

We were nervous – who wouldn't be – but we knew that Richard Barker and his team were with us and were now handling everything on our behalf. They gave us confidence and it was their experience that would count.

We still didn't know how we were going to be able to pull it off once we got to the Judicial Review. If everything relied purely on what we said against what Beyonce and Britney had said about the vials, who knew what would happen, but that was for another day.

One step at a time as Richard had told us.

Mum, Dad and I travelled by train from Doncaster to King's Cross and took a taxi to the High Court in the Strand.

When our taxi pulled up outside the building the whole experience felt surreal.

It was one of those jaw-dropping, 'Oh My God' moments. You see national television reporters talking of all kinds of cases outside of the High Court, but us? Our little case about our little bull! I know Boxy's a very big bull, but you know what I mean.

That's when it suddenly occurred to me, 'What the bloody 'ell are we doing here?'

We were all in awe of this huge, impressive building and

what this place was all about. This is where, since 1875, every major court case has been heard. We walked through security, which was understandably tight and much scarier than when you walk through airport security and found where we were to go, amongst what appeared to be hundreds of courtrooms.

We met Richard Barker and Dermott. Having spoken with Dermott many times over the phone in the past few months this was the first time we'd met him in the flesh.

Richard and Dermott were there before us and everyone was formally introduced. Dermott pointed in the direction of a much larger group of people around the corner from us, there must have been about ten of them, and mouthed that it was DEFRA's legal team so to be careful with what we said. We hadn't known who to expect, but there was no Clare Taylor, Beyonce, Britney, Crispin.

The hearing involved only one party speaking from each side. Stating our case was barrister Daniel Stilitz QC of 11KBW based at Temple in London.

On DEFRA's side was barrister Julie Anderson of 20 Essex Street chambers. Our Deputy High Court judge presiding was Mr Rabinder Singh QC. Neither Richard nor Dermott spoke.

Richard sat with us, which again was reassuring.

'We had thought that our barrister Peter Oldham would be putting our case. He had handled previous injunctions for us, but he couldn't make it. I just thought, "Here we go again, something else against us." Then when I first saw Daniel I thought, a bit like when you talk about all the policemen looking younger these days, he's a bit young. He looked only around his mid-30s and I wondered what experience he could have had. But I needn't have worried at all. He was excellent, a very impressive young man.'
  Anita Jackson

'I'd never been in anything like it in my life. I thought, "This is what it's come to," and shook my head in amazement. Things started to sink in when I saw the building. I still thought we were in the right, but

it made me think what have I done here? Local talk had been along the lines of, "Bloody 'ell Ken, going to High Court to fight DEFRA!"'

Ken Jackson

The case was scheduled for two hours but it took between three and a half to four hours. The format was that Dan would put our case, Ms Anderson would then put DEFRA's and then Dan was allowed a response.

We were very impressed with Dan. He put across our case superbly well. He was 'fab' is what I'd normally say.

When Ms Anderson spoke I felt that some of the stuff she was saying was so incorrect. That's when I started to find things frustrating because we couldn't say anything. Mum and I just sat there scribbling notes and passing them to Richard. He read each one and each time gave us a nod as though Dan had it covered. His reassurance and calm authority was really good for us. If we'd have just been sitting there I'm sure I'd have wanted to blurt something out and then got myself a reprimand from the judge.

One of the technicalities that DEFRA had tried to make a play of when we had Jacksons representing us was that we were 'out of time' for a Judicial Review, on the basis that there was a set period of time which we had to apply. We had been aware of this and had stated our case through Jacksons that the reason why this had happened was down to what we saw as DEFRA's delay in response from Andy Foxcroft months earlier.

It was a technicality, not the main issue, but we started feeling that the judge may have started warming to her point. He hadn't said anything, but his body language gave me the impression that he was going with Ms Anderson here. I suddenly felt that we might not be awarded the Judicial Review after all.

Looking at it from her point of view, she was simply battling on behalf of DEFRA. She wanted to win just as much as Dan, but my nerves were starting to shred once again.

That's when Dan stood up and pulled it out of the bag for us. We had done our homework with Richard and Dermott beforehand. Dan had been properly briefed so he knew what was coming. He had the answers that the judge was looking for over this point. He talked about the letter from Andy Foxcroft and the 'out of time' issue. He was careful not to blame Jacksons. All he said was that they (Jacksons) had been under the impression the case was still in negotiation during this time.

The judge gave us the verdict. He ruled that we had 'an arguable case' and ordered that our bid to overturn the bull's death sentence should be heard at the court as a matter of urgency.

His words, reported in the *Daily Mail* were: 'This bull is a much-loved animal. He is a prize animal and it would appear that his value to these claimants is not simply to be assessed in monetary terms.'

Yes! We had won the right to a Judicial Review.

What happened next was like something you see on television and in films. The press were there in force – *Daily Mail*, *Daily Mirror*, *Daily Express*, quite a few of them. They were all firing questions and we were like startled rabbits. We had just celebrated amongst ourselves and were bound for the nearest pub when suddenly we had all of this.

That's when Richard took control. He stepped in front of us and put up his hand like you see in films and told them: 'My clients will need a moment to reflect on the decision and they will share a statement with you, but please respect their privacy at this moment.'

It was something along those lines and I was thinking, 'Go Mr Barker!'

Once we'd got our act together we went back out to face the press. Dad and I both spoke and the *Daily Mail* reported that: 'Mr Jackson claims "they (Animal Health) could have avoided this if they'd only agreed to re-test Boxy" which he even offered to pay for.'

I was quoted as saying: 'We just don't believe the test was carried out correctly, according to DEFRA policy, and therefore we feel the result cannot be valid.'

After we had answered a few questions Dermott stepped in and told them enough was enough.

The pub was beckoning. Richard and Dermott came across with us. Dad was getting the drinks in whilst I was standing outside the pub on the phone giving the news to Paul, Andrew, Alan and Vera.

Dad came out to speak with Paul on the mobile.

'Paul said, "How have you got on?" and I said, "There's good news and bad news." He said, "What's the bad news?" I said, "The ale in this pub is terrible." So he guessed what the good news was.'
Ken Jackson

It was a great day. Our best day for months.

Chapter 25

Livelihood at Risk

We had finally been granted the Judicial Review. I know it makes it sound as though this was what we had wanted all along, but really it wasn't. All that we had wanted was that second chance for Boxster because of the botched blood test back in April 2010.

We hadn't wanted to go to court, but that was the only choice we had. We had been done an injustice by the girls – Beyonce and Britney – who had lied about their bungled attempts at collecting Boxster's sample.

Our only problem was that if it really did come down to the girls' words against ours, how would the judge see it? We didn't have anything else.

Sure, we could add the contamination issue of mixing vials and write all sorts of reports, but if the judge had already taken a stance against us and favoured the girls' version of events this wouldn't even come into play.

These were just some of our thoughts, but now that we had been granted the Judicial Review it was time for other factors to be properly taken into account.

If ever there was a time for soul searching this was it.

Fighting an injustice is one thing, putting your whole family at risk whilst trying to prove a point is another. I knew that there were financial pressures I was putting on my brother Paul that were particularly unfair on him. He was in an impossible position. He didn't have the same attachment to Boxster that I had, yet he was the one who ran the farm with Dad, and kept the business going with his wood-chip enterprise.

Paul would have been absolutely justified in putting his foot down and telling us that this farm was his livelihood just as much as anyone else's, and definitely far more so than mine.

Andrew ran his own successful business and I was employed elsewhere. What right had I to force Paul down this path?

It would be easy here to say that Mum and Dad wanted to see this injustice sorted and to show the girls up as liars, but I'm level-headed enough to know that part of the reason why they stuck with this so much was because seeing your daughter in tears is always a powerful driving force.

But now we really had to consider the cost of all of this.

It had already been reported that DEFRA had spent over £50,000 up to this time. We had already spent more than Boxster's valuation of £20,000.

We were way past that. If we were going to take this right through to its natural conclusion – and lose – we would be seriously messing with our well-being.

It's all very well sticking to your principles, but if the result was to be that we were to make life uncomfortable for the rest of Mum, Dad and Paul's lives, did we really want to go through with it?

It was only once we had returned home from the hearing that we found out roughly how much we were looking at having to pay for our Judicial Review in the High Court.

Our barrister fees for two days would be £40,000.

We nearly fell through the floor. If we wanted reality to smack us right in the face this was it. What's more, that was just the barrister fees. Solicitors' fees were on top of that.

Barker Gotelee were making sure we knew everything we were getting into. They told us that DEFRA's cost for their barrister would be identical to ours, and once again we needed to add solicitors' fees. They told us that we would have to pay for all of that too if we lost.

I know Mum was worried now. She handles all of the finances for the farm even though the only time she gets talked about in the press – and partly here – is for baking cakes and putting on wonderful spreads!

'I've got to admit that I was the one who said, "Gosh, are we doing the right thing?" That's when I started thinking like Paul.'
Anita Jackson

'We would never have been able to even think of taking this on if we'd been a tenant farm. It was only because we had assets that we could afford to talk about selling to raise money. We were still fattening cattle, but things were getting a bit tight and we were having to borrow money from the wood-chip business. I remember ringing the accountant and saying that it looked as though we would have to sell land. We couldn't afford to pay £100,000+ out without doing something like that.'
Ken Jackson

I spent a lot of time sitting on my own, thinking things through, getting emotional but also getting real about all of this. I just kept thinking about what I was doing to Mum and Dad and Paul. They were risking everything here if we went through with it.

I knew it was me driving the whole thing because Dad had always said, 'What do you think? What do you want to do?' And he had gone with every decision I had made. But this was big. It was no longer about whether we would win or not. The money side was now major.

It seemed like everyone was worried for us and particularly for Mum and Dad. I could understand that and it was killing me inside. I wanted so much to see this whole thing through and win but I knew that the others had more than a point.

Vera didn't think we should take it on. Paul, understandably, didn't want us to put his livelihood at risk and cripple the farm for him, Mum and Dad.

'I was worried because if we had to pick up these massive bills we

would have to sell some land. The thing that stuck in my mind was that (although we had the assets in the land) Mum and Dad had never really had a great deal. If they were going to sell land it should have been so that they were going to have a better standard of life, not to pay off debts they didn't need to take on. To me it looked like they might be throwing money away.'

Paul Jackson

Around this time Alan came over from Darlington to chat things over with Dad about the case and other Blonde Society stuff. Dad always valued his opinion and they were best friends. Carol came with him.

Dad asked Alan for his opinion of what we should do and Alan told him he thought we would be crazy if we carried on. He said we should let Boxy go because it was too much of a risk.

Carol could see how the thought of letting Boxster go still affected me and suggested we go and look at the pups one of my dogs had. Alan came too.

We chatted pleasantly enough then Carol started talking about Mum not being well and Dad not sleeping very well. It's true.

Mum suffers from what is called primary biliary cirrhosis, it's a chronic liver disease. There is no cure. It is commonly found in Scandinavia, Scotland and North East England and is not due to excessive alcohol consumption as most people think when they hear the word cirrhosis. It's your immune system attacking your liver.

Dad has not slept well in years. We have suffered a few family traumas over the years, not least when our cattle were being poisoned by ash deposits near our land. The financial stress as well as mental stress caused can be contributory factors.

Carol was worried that the stress of the court case, especially the fear of losing and having to pay out a huge sum, might affect Mum and Dad too much. I knew what she was saying and that she was trying to get me to let go of Boxy.

Alan and Carol both then told me that Dad was only

carrying on because of me and that I was the one who could stop it. They said that whilst ever I kept it going that Dad would never give up.

I knew it was true. I know that the saying 'daughters always have their fathers wrapped around their little fingers' is right. And I also knew that so long as I kept believing, he would do the same.

I'd known Alan and Carol were right about what they were about to say before they came. I knew it even more once they had gone. Only best friends can tell you what really hurts most.

Barker Gotelee had been patiently waiting for our decision. They were wanting an answer.

Mum was in the office; Paul was working. Dad and I sat in the room where all the decisions had been made. We'd had all the advice we could possibly have wanted and we both now felt that we shouldn't go ahead with the Judicial Review.

We were both at the point where rational thinking had brought us to the conclusion that we were done. It was over.

It was too much of a risk. I still didn't say the words that Carol, Alan, Vera and Paul were probably urging me to. I couldn't bring myself to that. But in my head I knew that we had to stop.

Suddenly Dad slammed his arm on the chair and said, 'Right, let's have a whisky.'

There are times writing this book when I feel that a distillery would benefit from using us in their advertising campaign! Quite possibly one named after a well-known game bird!

The bottle came out and we both had a good slug of it. We sat, more or less in silence. I was trying hard to hold back the tears, but it was useless.

Then he said those familiar words, the ones I knew that meant he would go with whatever I said.

I didn't want to go against everyone else. I didn't want to put everything at risk, and I tried hard not to say, 'Yes, let's fight them.' I just said that I hated the fact that they were going to win whilst they were telling lies. Why should we lose what we'd been fighting for because they had made a mistake?

It was all based on lies. We'd gone all this way because two people didn't tell the truth about mixing blood samples. I didn't think they would have got the sack if they had come clean about it, but for whatever reason they didn't. That's why it had snowballed from there. Now we were in this stupid position. That's what was making me angry. I didn't want them to get away with it.

'So what do you want to do?' he asked me again. This time I said, 'No, I'm not making that decision. This is your livelihood.'

I could almost feel a chorus of 'Hallelujahs' going up in the wood-chip building; at our neighbours, Vera Gresty's; and at the Hall's up in Brafferton, near Darlington.

Dad took a second. He then said: 'Bugger it, give me the phone. We'll go for it.'

And he rang Dermott there and then.

He told him: 'We're going to court, we're not packing in.'

Kate with Boxy – Supreme Champion at
Halifax Show 2009.

Kate and Boxy at Halifax Show 2009 – signs
of my fibromyalgia with splints on my wrists.

Boxy & Kate just before Boxy
was isolated for 18 months.

Boxy in Jail –
in his isolation
pen.

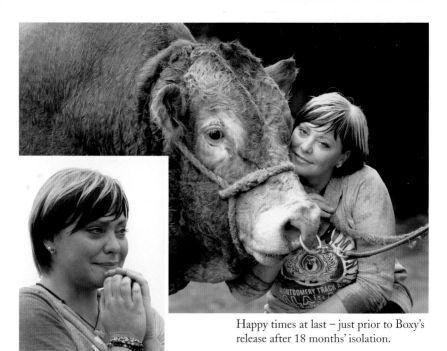

Happy times at last – just prior to Boxy's release after 18 months' isolation.

My tears of joy as Boxy returned to his ladies.

Boxy bucking and skipping with joy at being released.

Boxy on the charge, back with his family.

How Boxy used to come to me for a cuddle.

Boxy grazing on the hill at Womersley where he would come flying down to greet me.

Kate with Boxy getting ready for the book launch in 2012 at Forlorn Hope.

Kate with Boxy – talking with visitors to the original book launch in 2012 at Forlorn Hope.

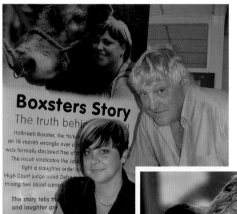

Kate and Ken at the official launch of *Boxster's Story* at Selby Livestock Market.

Front cover pic of *Boxster's Story*.

Boxy in the background with his daughter Stubbs Walden Fern plus two granddaughters.

Boxy's fame spread right across the world – here with David Huang of Taiwan.

Boxy as a grand old man laid in the sunshine at Wrancarr Mill in 2016.

Boxy – the grand old man, with his magic powder.

Kate with Dora – Supreme Show Champion at Driffield Show 2014.

Kate with Blonde cow Dora and heifer calf Katem Justice at Emley Show 2014.

Kate and Jewel – Supreme Champion at Great Yorkshire Show 2015.

Andrew with 'Mi Julie' at Wrancarr Mill

Kate with Katem Le Kracker – Male & Junior Champion at Lincolnshire County Show in 2016.

Boxy daughter Justice at Nottinghamshire County Show in 2016.

Kate showing Katem La Karole at Honley Show 2016.

Boxy's son Katem McAlan, named after Alan Hall, Male and Junior Champion at Lincolnshire County Show in 2017.

A Boxy granddaughter.

A Boxy granddaughter Katem McNita born 2016 and named after my mum.

Boxy's ashes in a wicker basket inside Alan's show box – with his wife Carol's number plate.

Boxy's tag number – now my bracelet.

Katem herd logo.

The Katem herd grazing at Wrancarr Mill in 2019.

Chapter 26

Sample 54

We had made the decision.

Despite all the warnings, the probability of failure, financial undoing and additional stress this would bring, we were going ahead.

By now we were receiving even more media attention. Boxy's story was covered on television and radio.

Patrick and Gemma were getting quizzed at school about what was going on as their friends had seen me on ITV and BBC news.

We were also receiving support from those who had been touched by the reports.

'We received one letter of good wishes just marked BOXSTER THE BULL, SELBY. And it got here. The phone calls and letters were unbelievable.'
Ken Jackson

'We had customers ringing to order wood chip who asked how we were getting on with Boxster. They all gave us 100% support.'
Paul Jackson

We still had a lot to do. We were now at what football and rugby league teams call 'the business end' of the journey. The court case was looming and we needed to go through everything. All of our witness statements needed writing. They included mine, Dad's and the lads – Melvin and John. They told me what they wanted to say and I typed them up for them. Mum was helping with it too.

Every element of our claim was analysed, double- and triple-checked. We knew that this was the time for going through everything with a fine toothcomb, to make sure everything was as it should be. It was vital that our solicitors had grasped everything that we had told them, everything had to be spot on, there couldn't be any gaps or loopholes for DEFRA to exploit.

Our problem remained the same. When it finally came down to making a decision over whether the judge would call in our favour the main issue would be who he believed.

There was no evidence as such. We could talk as much as we liked about contamination, but before that was an issue the judge had to be convinced that Boxy's blood samples had been mixed.

Professor Torgerson was doing all he could. His scientific reports about bovine TB and about contamination issues would be useful, but we knew that we could do with something else.

And that's when we found the most important and trial-breaking piece of our jigsaw. It came from DEFRA!

In preparing for the High Court both sides request information from each other.

DEFRA were coming up with arguments for their defence and we were having to give our arguments against. They appeared to have three scientific experts on their side, we had just one.

We had to go through all of their papers, which were a bit mind-boggling. We noted what we felt were contradictions all the way through their reports. Then we would email Dermott to show him our findings. It was a tortuous process, but we stuck at it.

Dermott then sent it through. The case-breaker!

The document that provided us with evidence that Beyonce and Britney had been lying all along showed all of the ear tag numbers of every animal that was blood tested on 7 April 2010.

By the side of each ear tag number there was a sample

number, which was in the numeric order that Beyonce and Britney had used. The sample number therefore linked each animal inextricably.

When we first looked at the document, which was about four or five pages because it was a list of all the animals blood-tested that day, we were downcast.

Dermott's note that came with the document had also been downbeat. The gist of his note was that we looked pretty stuffed if this was right. He'd looked at the document himself and he was concerned that what the girls said had happened on the day looked as though it could be borne out by this.

When we looked at the detail – and as well know, that's where the devil is – we knew instantly they were covering it all up. And how they had done it!

The sampling list showed that Boxster's was the third sample. There was no note of any half sample or anything untoward. A downright lie!

DEFRA's claim was that Vinnie was due to be the second animal they tested on the day.

They claimed that it was Vinnie that had been the animal that had played up and that they couldn't get a sample from. Another downright lie!

They claimed that Boxy was the third animal they tried and they got a sample from him with no problem. Another downright lie!

We knew it was all lies!

Come on! Hallelujah!

When I looked at the sheet again it showed that the first to be tested on the day was Nectarine. That was correct. The sample number ended 51.

Sample number 52 was missing. Sample number 53 was Boxster.

To anyone who had not been involved and only heard DEFRA's version of events it all seemed very reasonable, but we knew that Vinnie couldn't possibly have been attempted.

Firstly, he was right down at the other end of the yard. Why would they test Nectarine next to the crush, and then move down to the end of the yard for the second test only to move back to the crush to test Boxster?

They were using the missing number 52 sample, which we knew had been wasted on Boxster, as though they had attempted to test Vinnie.

They were using our own words about Vinnie, that I had mentioned to them on their arrival, to make up a story about him playing up. Another downright lie!

I didn't think for one minute that either of the girls had it in for us. They really had been 'right enough girls' like Dad had said. I could only speculate that somewhere along the way, when things got hairy with us challenging DEFRA, that perhaps the girls had come clean with their bungling over Boxster's sample.

Perhaps by this time maybe someone at Animal Health felt that they were in too deep to go back and that they needed to concoct a story. One way or another it was certainly some form of fabrication. Downright lies!

But how could we prove anything?

Dermott and I talked. He reckoned we had a major problem here; that DEFRA were providing us with evidence that said they were right.

I was thinking the same.

The document corroborated both our story and theirs. The vial before Boxster's officially recorded blood test (52) wasn't there as we knew it wouldn't be, but DEFRA's cock and bull story about why it wasn't there was the killer.

It would be back to our word against theirs.

That's when Mum and I sat down and went through every animal sampled and every blood sample number. We looked at the groupings, the pens they were in, we sampled each pen in turn, and the groupings both around the crush to start the day and at the end of the yard.

We checked that all the pedigrees were recorded together, all the commercials, the young ones, the bulls. We felt there were a few discrepancies and wrote them down.

We were studying this document for hours.

Then we noticed something that was so obvious. Yes, 52 was missing. Yes, 53 was Boxy's. The next animal to be sampled after Boxy was Katie. That was the order we had said all along, because it was true. Nectarine, Boxster and Katie. But Katie's sample was 55.

That meant 54 was missing!

There had been no mention of another animal that Beyonce and Britney had trouble with after Boxster.

But both 52 and 54 were missing.

We couldn't believe we had missed this when we had looked at the document for so long, but there it was.

How could they explain the missing No.54? They hadn't made any attempt to explain it up until now and they knew our story. Three attempts, one vial mixed from two partial samples. We knew that the first one (52) had been a disaster, so they had clearly mixed the samples of the other two by adding sample 54 to sample 53. That's why Katie was sample 55.

We breathed a huge sigh of relief first, because it had looked as though this document had been the end of our road. But now we were excited.

This was actually the one piece of evidence that would back up our experience, what we had said all along and would seemingly undo DEFRA's lies.

I don't think DEFRA's legal team had noticed there was a sample missing after Boxster's. They certainly would have tried to concoct another story if they had because this was so damning.

They were probably too concentrated on Animal Health's original concocted story about Vinnie that when they found there was a missing sample before Boxster's sample they thought 'bingo' this matches with the girls' story!

In my opinion they either did not look at what happened with sample 54 or they hoped we wouldn't notice it.

We had bad news for them. We had noticed.

When we received copies of the statements from Beyonce

and Britney we were even more encouraged.

Their stories were so fabricated and didn't match. They had given their locations whilst the blood tests were undertaken, but they hadn't got those right either. They said that during the sample taking of Boxster that Dad wasn't present. It was another lie.

There was no way that Dad would leave myself and the two of them alone with a bull or any of his herd whilst a test like this was taking place.

There were far more points than these.

Mum and I picked right through every aspect of their statements and there were more holes in them than a colander. Beyonce had only ever been to the farm that one time and it showed. Britney had been twice. Their recollection of where they had stood, where Britney had moved to in order to keep safe and the geography of the yard and where all the animals were situated was a joke.

At one point I wished that we'd had CCTV installed, we would then have had full incontrovertible evidence of their lies.

In order to explain everything to Dermott I drew a map of the yard, including the position of all the animals, the pens, the crush, where every animal was tied if it wasn't in a pen, where we were all standing and where the girls were.

We also reconstructed the animals' positions and took photographs of them.

Nectarine was no longer with us and Boxy was in his isolation pen, so we used 'extras', and tied them in their places. We then sent all of our efforts – the map, the photographs, our reply to the girls' statements. We felt good. We weren't counting on winning just yet but we felt that our chances of the judge finding in our favour must surely now be greatly enhanced.

What the girls had failed to understand was that we knew our animals, and in particular the special ones including Nectarine, Boxster, Vinnie, Katie and Vi.

We knew exactly where they were and what happened to them.

They had failed to realise that the reasons they were tied in certain locations were for good reasons. Everything had a set pattern.

The girls clearly hadn't seen them as anything more than animals to be tested, numbers in their day. You could see that by their lack of empathy towards the animals when they were testing them.

Our animals have always meant far more than that to us. Dad could tell you the name of every cow, bull and calf.

Despite our spirits surging when we found out about vials 52, 53 and 54 from the blood test list we weren't letting up on anything.

It was hard to get the feeling out of our minds that we'd got them now, and that we'd finally been able to prove that we were right all along. But we still wanted anything and everything we could get.

Professor Torgerson would write a paper. Their three scientists would write against it. Then he would write and respond to all three. He really fought our corner.

His best 'find' was a published paper by Dr Vordermeier, who was writing scientific reports against us, where he had written about inaccuracies of the gamma interferon test. These inaccuracies seemed to contradict his statement relating to our case.

We were still trying desperately hard to find any supporting evidence, other cases, other farmers who had been in a similar position.

We found a couple of farmers. One was a chap who'd had a prize-winning pedigree cow. I found his case through constant Google-searching. He'd had a routine skin test and the only one that had been a positive reactor was the cow. He questioned the way the skin test had been taken and wasn't happy. They came back, re-tested. She went on to live!

That was interesting because we had been told that once an animal tested positive you couldn't change it. The reason given was that the skin had not been shaved properly. That was in

1997 and 'policy' hadn't changed since then. I passed his case on to Barker Gotelee.

I picked up another instance through a website called www.bovinetb.co.uk.

This site was also where we had picked up contact with Professor Torgerson. Their site states: 'We have researched the subject of bovine TB in depth and are concerned that the existing TB policy and testing system has major health and safety risks, is not sustainable, is too costly and is creating more problems than the disease it is supposed to be controlling/eradicating. We are concerned that it is now more about achieving political targets and meeting deadlines than safeguarding animal and human health.'

One specific story I picked up from the website spoke of a lady's special animal that had shown up as a positive reactor. She had questioned the test as she didn't know how it could be that she'd had a reactor. Her herd was a closed herd, she hadn't been anywhere with it and she wasn't in any kind of TB area. She had to have it slaughtered. DEFRA gave her a hard time and wouldn't let her see any paperwork.

This lady had serious legal experience herself and quoted various pieces of legal jargon at them, notably the Freedom of Information Act, so they agreed to let her have a tour of the laboratory where the sample had been taken and analysed. They showed her the results of her herd on a computer but wouldn't let her have a print-out.

She sent me the notes from her meeting.

One of the people she had met was Dr Vordermeier. As soon as I saw his name I wanted to know more. DEFRA had explained to her the process the samples went through. She was shown her herd's results on their computer.

When she looked at the result of her cow, that they had said tested positive, the result shown was a negative. She questioned it and was told that someone must have hit the wrong key on the computer!

Human error happens is how they explained it to her. I

believe she received some form of compensation.

What had interested me particularly was that Dr Vordermeier had explained something that the DEFRA laboratory people had done was just human error.

Beyonce and Britney's actions were surely human error too?

I sent all of this information on to Dermott. We thought we had DEFRA now, that we had a case as Richard Barker had said months before, but we weren't leaving any stone unturned.

We didn't want them to have a ghost of a chance.

Chapter 27

Ghostbusters

I could feel Dad cringing when this chapter appeared in the first book, so I'll say it again so that he knows it was all about me. This next strange bit, to many, was my idea.

I'd been going for the odd massage to a girl who was very spiritual. I like that kind of thing. We spoke about this ghost team that was operating in the area. I had been telling her about what was going on.

My masseuse told me that this team would come out for free and see whether there were any negative spirits on the farm.

After all we had been going through and the hours we had put in, going back and forth through our case, I just thought this was something different for a night regardless of what happened. I really, truly was trying everything!

They arrived on a Saturday evening. There were three of them, two ladies and a man. I didn't know what to say to them. What do you say to a ghost team?

They said they would start in the farmhouse. They wanted to visit every room. Linda, who was the leader of the trio, asked if I would like to come around with them and whether I would like to carry one of their pieces of kit. They had cameras, camcorders, electric meters that pick up something or other.

I took hold of a camcorder. We started by moving into the sitting room first. I put the lights on as we went in. That was my first mistake. 'No, we do it in the dark,' was what they said.

They started talking together about what they could sense. Linda said she could sense someone male. We all went upstairs where they felt the energy was really bad.

They felt what they said was the spirit of a farmer who had once lived here. They reckoned it was him who kept stopping Dad from having a good night's sleep. We then went into the farmyard, into each farm building in turn, and then to Boxy.

The ghost team night was a useful diversion from the rest of the stuff I'd been going through. It was all bizarre, as you might expect, but it was interesting as much as it was odd.

Funnily enough my dad slept better after they had been!

Chapter 28

In the Zone

The trial had been set for Thursday 17 and Friday 18 March 2011, and in the lead-up we were inundated with support. Letters arrived, phone calls kept coming in from all around the country.

Chris Benfield at the *Yorkshire Post* had followed our progress. He kept our story bubbling along. Dad had wanted to keep it that way, he didn't want anyone to forget, and that's what inspired much of the response we were getting.

You might think that we were getting some kind of buzz from being in the media spotlight. Well, we may have done in normal circumstances.

If it had been because of the right reasons, Boxy winning every show he entered in 2010 perhaps, then it would have been different but we were too focused on what we were trying to achieve.

We wanted it to stay in the public eye.

Our solicitors' advice was to keep things low key and not conduct interviews in case we jeopardised the case, but we wanted the support. It helped us through.

We listened to our solicitors and only gave just enough information to keep everyone interested.

We had thought that the more coverage we received the more Animal Health wouldn't like it and may have backed down.

We had people telling us they were saying prayers for Boxster every night before going to bed. And others were racking their brains over how they could help.

'Paul's father-in-law, Colin, kept coming to look at Boxster. He came up with the idea that if anything went wrong he and I ought to put

Boxster in a trailer, take him up into the Highlands and let him go. He said they'd never find him!'

Ken Jackson

It was manic in the days leading up to the Judicial Review.

. We were trying to make sure we'd covered everything.

When I was going for a walk, watching television, whatever I was doing, my brain kept working, going over things. Colleagues at work told me later that sometimes they felt as though they were walking on eggshells around me because I was obviously stressed. I found out later that I had been a nightmare to work with during the case. And that had personal repercussions for me later. If only DEFRA knew what they had done to our family, what they had put us all through!

I thought I had been putting on some kind of mask, that I'd been covering it well at home and at work, but I don't think it can have been as good a mask as I'd hoped.

I knew that at home I had become more short-tempered, not as tolerant and a bit touchy. By this time my own illness – fibromyalgia – had properly kicked in and I was in a great deal of pain. I was suffering a lot of spasms and twitches.

Andrew is always so protective. I knew he was concerned about what this was doing to me, but he let me get on with it because he knew I couldn't and wouldn't give up.

Probably deep down I felt that we couldn't do this, we couldn't have got this far and certainly not taken on DEFRA in the High Court. But I never wanted to let anyone else into that doubt. I saw that as weakness and if I showed too much and let people know I was worried that would make me question myself even more over whether I was right to carry on.

I still felt guilty more than anything, guilty about what I felt I was putting Mum, Dad, Paul, everyone through.

But when we had made that final decision to 'go for it' in court, when Dad had said 'bugger it!' I had clicked into automatic pilot mode.

I know I can be stubborn and headstrong. I can feel Mum,

Dad, Paul and, of course, Andrew nodding as I write this, but we had got so close that there was now no way anything was going to stop me.

I was in the zone.

The thing was, were we going to be able to pull it off in the zone that mattered – the High Court of Justice?

Chapter 29

The Judicial Review (Day 1)

This was the big one. And we also knew that this time it wouldn't all be down to two barristers fighting against each other.

At the hearing in January the judge had granted permission for witnesses to be heard.

Being on oath was okay by us, we had nothing to hide.

We prepared ourselves in case we were called to take the stand. On the way down to London, on the train, we went through everything. We had brought all of our research, documents, photographs, statements, the lot. Our table and seating was just a mass of files.

Dermott and I exchanged a number of emails as we travelled, before my laptop finally gave up!

Once we'd reached our hotel in Russell Square, which wasn't the best, I caught up with any loose ends. I worked through the night going over and over it all again in my head.

When we reached the High Court we found that we were now in one of the upstairs courts.

That's when it hit us again. These courts were much bigger than where we had been the first time. They oozed authority. We had gone up another notch in the legal system.

But we were to get what you could take to be a little sign of fate, especially if you're in any way superstitious, just before we went into our courtroom.

There were statues outside each courtroom, but our statue was probably the most fitting it could have been.

It was named after General Wolfe who fought the Battle of

Forlorn Hope in Quebec, the battle that our farm was named after. It couldn't have worked out better in a novel let alone our very real story. I saw it as a good sign.

As we waited to enter the courtroom a posse of Animal Health people, their legal team and their witnesses arrived. Beyonce and Britney, and for the first time since we had seen her at Selby Livestock Market nearly a year earlier there was Clare Taylor.

There were so many of them to our meagre number that it scared me a bit, but I still had faith in our case. Especially with the number 54.

We were called in.

Everything about this courtroom was impressive and also very intimidating. This was where major cases had been heard. The Honourable Mr Justice McCombe appeared. The case was summarised by a court official.

It wasn't long before we had our first taste of the judge's opinion.

He wasn't happy with the way in which documents had been presented from DEFRA, nor the way in which DEFRA and their legal team had approached both the case from a legal point of view, nor the way DEFRA had dealt with us.

The following quotes were reported in the *Yorkshire Post* story 'Judge goes on rampage as farmer stakes last claim to save his prize bull':

A judge today attacked the "strident manner" in which Government officials and lawyers are calling for a prize-winning bull in Yorkshire to be destroyed after testing positive for bovine TB.

'Mr Justice McCombe said the case presented to the High Court on behalf of the Department for Environment, Food and Rural Affairs (DEFRA) was giving the impression "we know best – the nanny state knows best".

'The way some documents had been presented "just raises the hackles, I am afraid", said the judge.

'At the start of today's hearing, Ms Anderson opposed moves by the

farmers' lawyers to call oral evidence and cross-examine witnesses, including DEFRA technicians who conducted the test, to support their case that Boxster's blood samples had been mixed.

'As she made her submissions, the judge told her: "I don't like the strident manner in which this case is being put from the beginning."

'The judge said the DEFRA case "might be right – might be wrong" in its arguments, but there was evidence of "increasing anger and stridency" in DEFRA documents before the court that was "wholly misplaced".

'He was also extremely concerned over the way DEFRA was putting the case simply as "black and white", which it definitely was not. "It is a difficult matter", said the judge.

'Ms Anderson said if that was the position, it was entirely her error – "I am sorry I have done that".'

Yorkshire Post, Thursday 17 March 2011

It felt like a good start. Justice McCombe had said exactly what we had felt since this whole process had started. And we still had our 'ace' to play over the mixing of the vials.

Dan (Stilitz) said he believed cross-examination of witnesses was necessary.

All I could think when the judge was asking whether witnesses were needed was 'please still go to cross-examination'. I wanted to see the girls get up there on oath. The judge agreed.

Within what seemed a split second he asked for the first witness to be called.

They called me!

We had gone from getting permission to have witnesses, to going up in the stand. It was like Bang!

My knees went to jelly, I felt sick, Dad stood up to let me go to the stand. All I kept saying to myself was that it didn't matter what they threw at me because I know that what I would be saying was the truth.

I took the bible in my right hand, just as you see on the television.

Ms Anderson stood. She had two big green files. I had

been given a copy of them. She told me to turn to a page and a section. I was flicking through thinking, 'Oh my God, Oh my God, what have I missed?' I thought I'd covered everything. What had she found?

When I reached the section she had asked me to find it was the sheet with the ear tag numbers and sample numbers, the blood test.

She asked whether I recognised the sheet and then whether I would say that all the animals on the sheet had been tested in the correct order. I stopped for a moment and took a deep breath.

I was so concerned about saying the wrong thing. It's crazy really because you know you're telling the truth. I was concerned that anything I might say even slightly out of place might jeopardise everything we'd gone through.

What I said was that I couldn't possibly say that every animal had gone through in the order shown on the sheets. I told her and the judge that there were a lot of animals there, that I hadn't been responsible for the paperwork.

She came back at me asking whether, if I looked at it generally, I would say it was the right order or would I say there was something wrong.

I told her again what I had just told her. I then told her that I was on oath. I wasn't going to swear on oath that every single animal on there was tested in the order shown or not.

She asked several times. I replied that I couldn't tell her that every single animal was in the correct order on the sheets in front of us, but that what I could tell her was that I knew which order the first three animals had been tested.

She wouldn't give up. Justice McCombe stopped her. He'd heard enough.

Ms Anderson moved on. I thought she seemed a little deflated. I was becoming more comfortable. She asked a few questions that seemed irrelevant, but then she started to question the plan of the yard we had submitted. She asked me to draw where everyone was situated on a photocopy of the plan I had drawn up.

I knew we were on very firm territory here. We had discussed and checked everything. I did what was asked and that was it. Dan didn't question me. There was no reason. We hadn't lost any ground at all here.

I was a bit gutted really. I was into my stride now and this wasn't as daunting as I first thought it would be. I stepped down. Dad was next.

'I said: "I don't know what we're doing here, we never ought to have been here. We should be working together, not stuck in the High Court."'
Ken Jackson

Ms Anderson must have thought she could bully Dad, because that's what we felt she tried to do to him. She had asked him to turn to page number such and such. Dad flicked through, but he was in the wrong folder. He was fumbling about. He's a farmer for God's sake, Mum does the paperwork generally and I had done quite a bit of it for the case with Mum. I was still hoping he'd find what she'd asked him to look for soon.

She kept trying to hurry him up. The judge dressed her down. He told her that Mr Jackson was an expert in his field and that she should give him time to come to terms with hers. Finally, Dad found what she had asked him for.

What followed was pretty comical, but most farming families will find it amusing. It didn't seem at all amusing to Ms Anderson.

She asked him about a letter sent to Animal Health from Forlorn Hope Farm, and whether Dad had ever seen the letter before.

Dad said he hadn't.

She asked again. He said he'd told her he hadn't. She reminded him he was on oath. He looked at it again. She told him that it was a letter from his farm to Animal Health and what possible explanation could he give for not having seen it before?

Dad's answer will ring true with many farmers up and down the country.

He said: 'Well I didn't deal with any of the paperwork, our Kate did.'

It felt as though I could hear her jaw hit the floor. I didn't know whether she could call me back about this because I'd been up already. Maybe she'd missed her chance by questioning the wrong person. I don't know how many farming families she had cross-examined before, but I would lay odds that it is not many!

We never found out what she was going to ask as I wasn't recalled.

Ms Anderson then pulled out the plan of the yard again. I felt sure she was trying to catch us out with this. Dad had to go through the same exercise. He did as I had.

She then asked Dad about the telephone call with Crispin at Animal Health. It appeared as though she was trying to build a case around some nice words my dad had said about the test carried out by Beyonce and Britney, as if to say that we had been happy with them.

We hadn't been unhappy with the girls until the test results had come back, as we'd said countless times; in fact we hadn't been really unhappy with them until we found out about their lies. We had just accepted them as two girls going about their job and it had been quite a tough, challenging day for all of us, the girls included. Dad had quite rightly said nice things about them at the time.

She tried to remind Dad about the conversation he'd had with Crispin. Dad said that he recalled saying 'they were right enough girls' but that was about it. The judge, who I think was finding this reasonably funny, said that he could see Mr Jackson saying that. I think he may even have gone further by saying, 'That sounds right enough to me.'

That was it for Dad too. We broke for lunch, but not before Ms Anderson had hit us with another little problem. She now wanted to call John and Melvin, our two farm lads who had been helping with the cattle on the day of the blood test. We felt that since she may have thought she hadn't got very far with us she wanted another crack at somebody.

Lunchtime became panic stations!

They wanted John and Melvin, which meant we had to arrange everything double-quick. They had to be here first thing tomorrow. Now this might not appear too drastic to someone who is used to travelling but Melvin had very rarely been anywhere outside of a five-mile radius since he was born.

Dad had looked after him work-wise and home-wise for many years. He'd been in a few scrapes over the years. To get Melvin organised for anything takes time. We didn't have much of that and at first we couldn't even get hold of Paul to let him know the lads were needed. He was out delivering wood chip. We left messages with Paul and with Vera, who lives relatively close by. We went back into court.

Mum was praying that she wouldn't get called to the stand. When she was called I saw all the colour drain from her face.

'I found Ms Anderson intimidating. I think I fear women who are powerful more than men.'
   Anita Jackson

Mum was asked about ear tags and cattle numbers as well as the plan of the yard. Dan then asked Mum about the ear tag numbers of Nectarine and Boxster in preparation for later on.

Beyonce was next to the stand. She had been the one taking the samples. She seemed hesitant and to me she looked extremely worried. She had a tissue in her hand and was constantly touching her nose. Mum thought she had a cold. I thought this was classic body language that right now she needed some form of comfort.

Dan started questioning how long she had been in her role. It was years. He followed with a question about having carried out many bovine TB tests. The questioning led her to agree that she had probably conducted blood tests into their thousands.

That's when Dan said:

'So, what's the difference with Mr Jackson's farm that makes you so sure that you can remember it clearly and not get it confused with other farms you've been to in the past?'

It was a clever ploy. How could she be certain that the information she was giving was about our farm. Since she had been to so many?

Up until now we had been skating around the edges of the main issue. But the issue, the main issue of sampling and how it was conducted was next on Dan's agenda.

Beyonce was adamant that I had warned her of this dangerous bull we had – Vinnie. She had either misunderstood what I had said on the day or was purposely lying.

Vinnie had been a show bull. He'd been used to crowds. He'd had children ride on his back. We'd shown him for years. All I had done was warn her over his needle phobia and that it would probably be better to deal with him later as I'd tried to help by applying local anaesthetic cream.

She talked about a cow (Nectarine) and two bulls (Vinnie and Boxster) being tied next to each other. There was no way that Dad would tie two mature bulls side by side. Dan had told us that if there was anything that cropped up whilst he was cross-examining, that we wanted him to know, to write it down.

That's what we did here. It wasn't the last of our notes either.

Beyonce then told of how she had tested the cow (Nectarine) first. She then said that she had gone to the bull (Vinnie) who she said was kicking and thrashing about but decided that taking the sample was far too dangerous and would have put herself and Britney at risk, so she had refused to test him at that time.

I still could not believe they were now lying under oath!

Vinnie was at the other end of the yard and we were waiting for the local anaesthetic cream to take effect on his tail. She must have known this because Vinnie's results were much later. She also lied about where Britney had been positioned.

She talked about Boxster next and said that he had stood calmly. Lies, lies, lies! That's all I could think.

It was now that I just wanted to get up and shout just how much she was lying.

This is when Dan chose to ask her about the missing vials.

He got her to refer to the sheet of blood tests. He asked whether this was the sampling sheet that had been used on the day. She agreed it was. He asked whether she could see that there was a vial missing before the one they had recorded as Boxster's? She agreed that was the one she had used and discarded because the bull was thrashing about. Dan then said: 'So the animal tested after that, it was Boxster's vial?' Again she agreed.

The next moment was the one that we had been waiting for ever since we had noticed the missing vials either side of Boxster's allegedly full vial.

It was time for No.54 to reveal itself.

Dan said: 'We have a sample missing after Boxster's and before the next animal was tested, who was Katie (No.55).'

Now it was time for Beyonce's chin to hit the deck. Suddenly all their legal team began scribbling, flicking files and passing notes. They hadn't looked at this. It was new to them all. Someone would be for the high-jump after this.

'So,' Dan said for dramatic emphasis. 'Where did sample 54 go?'

She said she didn't know. Dan followed by saying that she had known where 52 had gone (the one she said she had discarded) and that she knew that 53 was Boxster's. So where had 54 gone? Again, she said she didn't know. She was clearly flummoxed by this.

He asked whether that could be the sample that the Jacksons said had been used to mix with 53 to put together one 'complete' blood test – a mixture of two vials?

Beyonce was becoming more agitated by now, her body manner giving her away so far as I was concerned. He asked how she could justify what happened to sample 54.

He pushed her until she finally said that she may have just put it into her pocket. It just made her look stupid. She had become increasingly nervous and twitchy.

The judge was certainly unimpressed with Beyonce's version of events where she tried to explain away sample 54.

She had given in evidence that sample 54 had come about from a tube that she had in her pocket as a spare, rather than following procedure. She said that using the tubes in a preordained sequence was not something that they stick to and it was 'not true that we have to do it.'

She also said: 'I could have had it in my pocket. I am behind the animal. I have it (the spare) to hand. I can put the new tube straight back on. I have one in my pocket for this. I must have had it.'

We felt that was one of the reasons why in note 26 of his judgment, the judge said: 'I am satisfied that the account given by Jacksons' witnesses is to be preferred to that given by Beyonce and Britney.'

Dan questioned her on other points, including the 'broken tail' incident. She tried to make out that I'd made a big song and dance about it and that it was all my fault. It was an exaggeration, and another lie, but I felt she had already done enough damage to their case.

But she could do a little more yet.

Dan had found out that Clare Taylor's 'full investigation' had consisted of nothing more than a ten-minute, three-way conversation with the girls. It was in their notes that this had taken place. They hadn't hidden it, but we felt it did hang them a little when Dan asked Beyonce if she had spoken to Britney prior to writing their witness statements and she had said she hadn't.

Ms Anderson chose not to ask her any questions. I don't suppose there was much she thought she could do with her!

Beyonce's time in the spotlight was the last act of the first day of the two that had been planned.

Dan was pleased with the way we had all come across and the way the case was going. He was looking forward to getting Britney on the stand the following morning. Mum, Dad and I walked back to the hotel in good spirits, but not wanting to take anything for granted. We had a chuckle about the way the judge had given Ms Anderson a ticking off right at the start and sample 54.

Meanwhile, back at Forlorn Hope, the action was about to get under way!

Chapter 30

Melvin & John Come to Town

Think of this next duo as our farm version of Cannon & Ball or the Chuckle Brothers!

'I couldn't get hold of Paul at all, so we'd tried Vera again. It was now around four o'clock. Vera answered and said she would nip round and tell Paul and the lads. We knew nowt more about what was going on back home until later when Vera said I'd given her a right job!

'It had only dawned on her, after we'd finished the call, that her car wasn't there, her husband had taken it. So Vera had got out her husband's bike. She'd not been on a bike for years and whilst I say she lived close it might have been close in a car, but not on a bike.

'What's more Vera, bless her and she won't mind me saying this, is quite a large lady and she's not really built for pedal pushing! She'd not been on a bike in years and she had to go a few miles. Her chain fell off a few times on the way too.'
Ken Jackson

'It had been bedlam that day. We had been absolutely pulled out. My phone was on charge. When Vera arrived it took her ten minutes just to get her breath back, and another ten minutes for me to understand what she was going on about. It was now about five o'clock. Vera had tried to make sure she got here before the lads had gone home and she'd only just made it in time. I then had to sort out train tickets so they could set off from Doncaster around six o'clock the next morning.'
Paul Jackson

'But that wasn't all Paul had to do. Melvin didn't have a suit or anything like it. Nothing smart enough for a court appearance. Another job for Paul.'
    Ken Jackson

'I said, "You're joking! I haven't got any gear. No suit." Paul took me to the Factory Outlet at Knottingley and bought me a new pair of shoes, trousers and tie. He picked the tie, he knew I'd pick the wrong one. Then he gave me one of his white shirts and a jacket. We did all the shopping in 20 minutes.'
    Melvin Burrows

'If we hadn't got sorted at the Factory Outlet there was always a charity shop next door! I'd told Dad there was no way I was taking him to Debenhams or Marks & Spencer.'
    Paul Jackson

After all of the rushing around from Vera and Paul the lads were on their way.

The furthest Melvin had been for the past 30 years was Knottingley and I'd never seen him wearing a tie. He looked the part as we met them the next morning at King's Cross. They were both quite jovial and were laughing about what had happened on the train.

Melvin had some really inappropriate Chubby Brown ringtone and it had gone off on the train, probably as a result of me ringing him to check they were okay. He told us the 'posh people' on the train hadn't been impressed, and he'd been 'effing and blinding' because he hadn't found it quickly enough to turn it off.

John had told us that he hadn't been able to take a step without Melvin being on his shadow as he'd been that concerned about getting lost in the big city. He had nearly lost him. And another thing. Melvin, believe it or not, had never been on an escalator in his life.

'I got on an escalator at King's Cross. Then I realised Melvin wasn't behind me. I looked back down and there he was at the foot of it not knowing how to get on. It was rush hour and he was holding up loads of people!'
   John Davison

But when they saw the building it was suddenly John who was overwhelmed.

'I just thought, "Bloody 'ell, this is a bit different to Selby Court." The size of the building made me nervous. It felt like I was going in to be tried for murder. The solicitor told me not to be concerned but I could feel my knees banging together. I was burning up.'
   John Davison

I'd been worried about Melvin and how he would be in court. I'd been on at both of them to read their statements over and over on the train. I hadn't been overly concerned about John.

'I didn't have my statement with me. I'd left it at home, but Kate had a copy and I read it when we got to London.'
   Melvin Burrows

So, there we were, all set for Day 2, with a nervous-as-hell farmworker who we thought was going to be okay before he saw the building; and another who looked better than we had ever seen him before, but who was only just checking over his statement. Brilliant!

Chapter 31

The Judicial Review (Day 2)

If the DEFRA legal eagles reckoned they'd had a bad day in court the first day, it was clear they intended to make up for it on the second.

But they had the wind taken out of their sails right at the start. It appeared to us as though Ms Anderson felt they needed something more, in fact anything more.

In addition to getting John and Melvin to come to town they now wanted to submit two new witness statements into court.

Both were based around this 'full investigation' Clare Taylor had apparently carried out, the one that Dan had so delicately brought into play yesterday.

It had proved a good move because now DEFRA's legal team suddenly wanted to submit a new statement from Clare Taylor and submit her as a witness.

She never took the stand. I was disappointed. I would have loved to see her squirm.

For the benefit of all, this is how Clare Taylor reported her findings from her 'full investigation':

'I was satisfied with the response of both (Beyonce) and (Britney) on the allegations. I spoke to (Beyonce) at her home by telephone and she had a clear recall of what had happened as Hallmark Boxster had been tethered separately with another bull and cow. (Britney) was sitting next to me in the office when I spoke to (Beyonce) and she corroborated (Beyonce's) recall.'
Clare Taylor, Animal Health

Miss Marple she was not!

The judge really dressed down Ms Anderson for trying to submit the new statements. He said something to the effect that she was not going to rewrite her witnesses' statements to bail out her witness from the previous day.

Strike One to us on Day 2!

When Britney walked to the stand I thought she looked every inch the star of some TV courtroom drama. She was fully made up, very smart, her hair in a pretty-looking ponytail and with a nice little tight skirt just above the knee.

As she went into the witness box she was very smiley, batting her eyelashes. I didn't think she could have laid all this on much thicker. Mum and I glanced at each other, we both felt the same.

Ms Anderson and her team had obviously been working hard on performance since yesterday. You could immediately see the difference between Britney and Beyonce in terms of confidence. Britney appeared well rehearsed and much more polished with her answers. To me she came across as very cocky to the point of arrogance.

Dan asked how long she had worked in her role.

She answered that it had not been long. He then quizzed her about the view she had of Beyonce conducting the sampling. DEFRA had been building part of their case around the fact that Britney had seen everything that Beyonce had been doing, particularly at the time Boxster's sampling had been undertaken.

We had known that where Britney had been standing meant that there was no way she could have seen what was going on. He asked whether she had a good view. Yes, she said, she did. She told him that she had positioned herself behind a gate because the samples were fragile and she needed to be in a secure position.

Dan asked whether she seriously considered the position she had mentioned. Whether it would have been secure, as she would then have been in a yard with loose cattle. I could see her confidence starting to drain away.

We knew she was either lying or couldn't remember where she had been standing.

Either way Dan tied her up in knots. When he finally asked how she could possibly see what was going on with Boxster as, from her answers she was positioned around a corner, she couldn't answer. She just shook her head.

She was done. She'd already lied about the sampling and the order it had been conducted. Britney walked away nothing like as confident as she had walked up.

It was time for our lads.

'I kept saying to them 'tell the truth', don't make anything up. If you don't know the answer tell her you don't know. I just felt that if they said something that wasn't quite right, but they'd said it just to give an answer, she would pull them up on it.

'The lads had been making fun of Melvin a few weeks before, telling him he might have to go to court – and here he was. He'd said back home, jokingly, "I'll tell that effin' judge that DEFRA is messing about with my job." The first thing I told him when he got down to London was, "Don't swear." I drilled it into him.'

Ken Jackson

'I was a bit scared, especially when I'd heard our guy cross-examining the girl with the ponytail. I didn't like the courtroom. I kept saying to myself, "Let me go home, I just want to go home." To be fair I didn't have a lot to say because I wasn't there when it was all kicking off. So it was really all down to John when he got up.'

Melvin Burrows

Melvin was called first. I'd told both of them that Ms Anderson would probably get them to mark where they had been on the day, on the plan.

All Melvin had done that day was lead Boxy up to the crush.

'When Melvin went on the stand Ms Anderson asked him what he had done at the day of the test. Melvin said he'd put a halter on Boxster and brought him. That he had led Boxster whilst I had brought Katie.'

Ken Jackson

'I told her that me and boss tied them up at the crush. Then boss told me to go bagging. Mr Jackson... Paul. Then she asked me who Paul was. I said he was other boss. She asked why I'd taken Boxster and Ken had taken Katie. I told her Boxster was quieter. I took the quiet one. After I'd done that I went off bagging.'

Melvin Burrows

The judge was intrigued. He asked what 'bagging' was. Melvin explained.

'Bagging? Stable-Dry!'

Another question from the judge: 'What is Stable-Dry?' Melvin thought everyone knew.

'It's bedding for horses!'

The way he said it came over as comical. Melvin couldn't believe people didn't know what bagging was. I don't quite know what Ms Anderson was hoping to get out of all this, but we were certainly having a laugh.

Melvin, even though he didn't know it, was doing great. He'd not sworn once! He'd been very polite. Ms Anderson asked him why he hadn't stopped with Boxster. Melvin was as matter-of-fact as he had been all along.

'Because boss told me I had to go bagging!'

If Melvin's testimony had been more like a stand-up comedy routine John's was all but that.

I've never been through anything like it in my life. I was so scared of saying something out of place and dropping us all in it. My throat dried up, the palms of my hands were sweaty, my hands were shaking and my knees were not just knocking, by now they were almost beating out a tune.'

John Davison

Unfortunately for John he was Ms Anderson's last hope of getting something useful to help her case and she was about to lay into him big style. She quizzed him about where he was when Boxster's sample had been taken and that he was sure he had seen the sampling.

She reminded him he was under oath and asked him to draw on the plan where he was at the time. When he had done this she had a smirk on her face. Either she thought she'd got something here, or she was trying to give the impression to the judge that she had.

All I could think of at that moment was, 'Oh no, what's wrong?' She then told him that the position he had put himself meant that he was standing behind myself and Dad, with us between him and Beyonce.

She asked if that was the case how he could clearly see everything. He started to say, 'Well yes, but...' and she jumped in. 'Let me remind you, you are under oath.' She was going for him big time now, but it wasn't because he was lying at all. He was scared out of his mind that he might have cocked things up. He was stunned and started 'umming and ahhing'.

I was just sitting there thinking, 'Take a look at him, he's far taller than me and Dad, he can easily see over the top of us, and you don't just stand in one position all the time, like a statue.' She was trying to prove we were lying, that one by one she could knock down the witnesses' statements.

She hadn't done it so far, but you could tell she reckoned she was getting close here. I was trying to send telepathic messages to John, to get him to calm down. She just kept pushing.

'All I could tell her was I didn't know anything other than I could see what was going on. I was a quivering wreck by the time she finished with me. I thought I had let everyone down, because before I'd had time to explain something she was on at me with the next question. It took me a long while to get over the experience. I just told Ken, Anita and Kate that I was so sorry, it felt to me like I'd blown it.'
John Davison

As John came back to sit with us, we knew he was upset, but we tried to reassure him that he hadn't messed up at all. He hadn't caved in and just given her the answer she was desperately searching for. He hadn't made something up. He'd stuck with the facts. But he was beating himself up about it for a long time afterwards. He couldn't think logically why he could see, he just knew he could.

The rest of the day was down to Ms Anderson presenting DEFRA's case. There were no more witnesses called.

The judge was keen to get it all wrapped up in the two days but their solicitors reckoned they needed more time. He tried to book another half day, but they pushed for a further two days. We didn't know whether they were doing it to make us back out because of the cost implications.

All we really knew was that this was still not over, but that we were pleased with how it had gone so far.

Dan had been fantastic. None of us had crumbled on the stand, not even John!

Chapter 32

The Judicial Review (Day 3)

The new court dates were set for Monday 28 and Tuesday 29 March 2011.

We had spent the intervening week and a half in limbo before returning to London to prepare for our next two days in court.

There was no evidence left to submit. We arranged to stay in a slightly better hotel than the first time, but still in Russell Square.

We had been reasonably happy ten days ago, the trial had gone well. But we didn't want to take anything for granted.

This time we were in a different courtroom once again. We no longer had General Wolfe outside our courtroom, but that didn't stop Mum and I from nipping up to touch his statue once again for good luck!

Dan met us before we went in with Dermott and Richard Barker. He told us that if there was anything we thought of during the proceedings we should jot it down and pass it to him.

I think he may have regretted saying that. I couldn't quite reach him apart from with my pen and ended up constantly prodding him with it.

When the case re-started it was Ms Anderson who stood up first. She was trying to hinge the case on the scientific evidence, presumably because she felt the testimonies of Beyonce and Britney had not been wonderfully successful.

Their evidence said that the mixing of vials wouldn't make a difference; ours said it would.

The judge said he felt the two sides' arguments balanced each other out and that he was not really interested in the science; he said he was more interested in what actually happened on the day and whether it made a difference or not.

Ms Anderson persisted and it appeared as though Justice McCombe was beginning to despair with her as he asked her to move on with her defence. He warned her that if she carried on it would not make a difference. She carried on with it.

At this point he gave up with her. He'd had enough.

He pushed back his chair, folded his arms and practically turned his back on her. She never batted an eyelid. She carried on carrying on with the science. She seemed to be going on forever.

When she eventually moved on from the science, she switched back to the sample mixing, which she still insisted was from a different animal. She was also adamant that a full investigation had been carried out.

Justice McCombe did not feel that a ten-minute, three-way telephone conversation constituted a full investigation and he told her so.

This all sounded as though we were still looking good, but then there would be times when we wondered why he seemed interested in other areas.

We felt Ms Anderson was now clutching at straws. She said there was no way, after all this time, that we could now prove that Boxster was bovine TB free.

But that would surely make a mockery of the four-yearly test? If, a year or so later, there was no test that Boxster could take that would say he was free of TB then why are there tests conducted every four years? It was another pen in the back moment for Dan.

At the end of Day 3 we didn't know what to feel.

The judge had dressed down Ms Anderson a few times, but we didn't know whether that was how every barrister behaved in her position.

Chapter 33

The Judicial Review
(The Final Day)

I'd had a bad night. My fibromyalgia, which is muscle and connective tissue pain, means my body swells up when it comes on and it makes me twitch.

Mum and Dad kept coming to my room to check on me. They tried to convince me to go home, but that was never on the cards!

I was not going to miss the final day.

But we were missing one of our team. Dermott had to attend another court hearing within the building for a short while.

Dermott had been making notes as well as Mum and I, so I tried to step into his shoes whilst he was away. I was now trying to come up with not just what we were thinking as the family but also like a solicitor.

When Dermott came back he laughed at the amount of papers on Dan's desk.

He said to me: 'Look how many papers you've written to Dan over the three days!' I told him that's just what I'd written since he hadn't been there!

Dan gave his summing up of the case. He was absolutely brilliant.

What I couldn't believe though was how rude the DEFRA legal team and their scientists would be during his summary. That's something you don't see in the movies. Dan would say something and each time there would be lots of gasping and shaking of their heads. I guessed their exaggerated body language was to attempt to sway the judge.

Dad kept having to stand up because he had a bad back; I was constantly jerking about because of the fibromyalgia; and the opposition seemed to be play-acting on their side of the courtroom.

It must have been quite a scene for Justice McCombe and I'm sure we would have found it hilarious had it not been so serious for us.

Justice McCombe asked Dan a few questions after he had completed his summing up. What was quite pleasing to me was that Dan used a lot of the notes I'd passed him.

It proved that it was worth all of our concentration. The judge seemed taken with our view over the four-yearly tests and the test accuracy. He asked Ms Anderson for a response. It wasn't forthcoming.

Both sides had now completed their cases.

If we had been expecting a verdict there and then we were to be disappointed.

I think we all thought that the judge would go into his chambers, have a cup of coffee and come back out in a few minutes, maybe half an hour, and then tell us his decision.

Naïve or what?

We didn't have a clue about how cases like this worked out. We were in the High Court. Justice McCombe hadn't got to where he is just to toss out verdicts that quickly. We might have thought it was an easy decision to make, but we hadn't reckoned on wider issues, such as the bearing our case may have had for future law suits.

Justice McCombe told us he had a great deal to consider and he had plenty to go through on the case before he could make a decision.

We were just concerned about winning.

He talked of precedents any ruling might set; he referred to human rights issues; policy interpretations; he even mentioned a famous case to do with a tribe being falsely imprisoned. He was looking at what the implications would be of any result.

So, after four days in the High Court and nearly a year's worth of fighting DEFRA, we were left a little deflated.

We asked Dan and Dermott how long it might take for Justice McCombe to deliberate and come up with his ruling. They said it could take months. We hadn't been expecting that.

By this point we had no way of telling how it would go.

Up until the summarising from the barristers we had thought we were getting close to the end; and that we had done pretty well. Now we were facing up to the possibility of something we hadn't planned on, an even longer wait.

It was an empty feeling. We'd done everything we could, but still we didn't know.

When we came out of court and went outside there were a lot of people buzzing around. There was one chap who came up to us with a camera. He said he was from the *Daily Mail* and asked whether we had won. He took a few snaps and that was it, we were done with London and the High Court.

This is how the *Yorkshire Post* reported it:

'The fate of Boxy, the prize-winning Yorkshire bull, hung in the balance today as a courtroom battle to save him from a death sentence came to a close. After many hours of legal argument, a High Court judge reserved his judgment. No date was given for Mr Justice McCombe's ruling on the fight over the future of pedigree bull Hallmark Boxster.'

Yorkshire Post – 29 March 2011

Chapter 34

The Singing Farmers

The Singing Farmers concerts used to take place every year around the end of March and beginning of April. Dad is one of six entertainers, along with Chris (Berry) who had been playing to big audiences around Yorkshire since 2004.

Dad has sung all his life, but the Singing Farmers concerts were different. They were all about the farming community and Dad, Chris, Tony, Charles, Phillip and Lloyd were well-loved for their annual tours.

In 2011 the concerts provided Dad with an ideal opportunity to tell a lot of the farming community what was going on with Boxster during his performance. It seemed that everyone was interested because as soon as the audiences started filtering into the respective halls and saw him it was the first question on their lips.

'Our first concert in 2011 was at Leyburn just three days after the end of the trial. I was 'capped' with how many people wanted to know. The second concert was at Malton on the same weekend and even more came up offering their best wishes. We really hadn't known just how much support there was for us out there. It was the same response at Brandesburton and Skipton the following week.'
   Ken Jackson

But Dad couldn't tell them how we had got on, because we still didn't know. What Dad did know, and that we were so grateful for, was that without his involvement with the Singing

Farmers we would never have had contact with Shirley Percy, the lady from RABI who had put us on to Richard Barker.

The concerts were a useful diversion from thinking too much about the result. They managed to fill some of the time between the trial in London and Justice McCombe's decision.

The Decision

Life carried on. Boxster stayed in his isolation pen. We had passed all of the skin tests since August and the herd was now TB free, but because of our dispute with DEFRA the farm was still quarantined. It had now been this way for so long that we had started to consider it normal.

Vera, our very own legal expert from her days in the police force, had told us it would need to be a brave judge to rule in favour of us because of the precedent it would set. Government departments don't like precedents of this kind, she had told us. It might set every other farmer off against them over their tests.

The longer it took, the more I think we were all expecting the worst.

I had returned to work and had just come out from a teaching session when I looked at my mobile phone. There was a missed call from Mr Barker. He'd left a voice message.

'Kate, I need you to ring me as soon as possible. We've got the verdict.'

I rang back, my head was almost exploding by now. This time I got his answer phone message. I rang Mum and said that Mr Barker (Richard) had rung.

'I know. He's rung me,' she said.

'And…?' I said.

And with that she burst out crying. It seemed ages before she spoke again. When she did it came out as a squeak!

'We've won! They've gone with us!'
   Anita Jackson

That was it for me. I just couldn't stop crying, so now neither of us could really talk.

'Mr Barker had hesitated before he told me. When he said we'd won I held it together. I thanked him very much and he said it had been a pleasure. I just couldn't wait to let Ken, Paul and Kate know.

   'I shouted, "Yippee!" as I went down the yard to find them, punching the air as I did so. I was absolutely ecstatic. It was like this weight being lifted.'
   Anita Jackson

'When Mum told me my first reaction was, "Thank God for that." As far as I was concerned, we were going to be back to normal. We could get on with farming and what we do with the wood-chip.'
   Paul Jackson

'I felt like going down to The Shoulder (our local) and getting drunk!'
   Ken Jackson

I rang Andrew, but it wasn't official just yet, so we had to keep it all under wraps until the official announcement came through. I'm sure we all just wanted to shout it from the rooftops.

You might think that this automatically freed Boxster and also took our farm out of quarantine. Not a bit of it.

We had taken one giant step for man against DEFRA, but we needed a few more just yet to achieve it for mankind, or in our case for Forlorn Hope!

Chapter 36

Celebrations

I've said many times during this book, the first one and this, that the Jackson family knows how to celebrate and we were certainly not going to miss this opportunity.

There were still plenty of other things to sort out, but winning in the High Court versus a Government department who have bullied you, twisted your words and lied? Well, it had to be done.

On the morning of the official announcement – Thursday 14 April – our phones rang constantly. Newspapers, radio, television all wanted to get our story. We knew that Justice McCombe was set to make everything official around 9.30am.

There were cars parked outside with photographers, video journalists, newspaper journalists, broadcasters.

We received the call we were waiting for from our solicitors, in between fielding press calls. But before we faced the media, whose numbers were growing outside our farm gate, Dad said:

'Right. We'd better get the whisky out!'
    Ken Jackson

This was 9.45 in the morning!

All the lads sat on the wall in the yard, everyone had a nice slug of whisky, Mum and I were just so happy and the lads were all very cheery.

Then we made our way around to the media. All of the BBC local radio stations had sent someone, because we're in an area where BBC Radio York, Leeds and Sheffield all broadcast; BBC TV's Look North programme wanted to film us with Boxy; the *Yorkshire Post*, *Farmers Guardian* and a number of the national press were all at the farm.

Look North were going to take our story as a 'live' event from the farm. I was in a fun and cheeky mood by now. Their presenter was a really lovely girl. She was running through her script and then I heard, 'Going live in 10, 9...'

I was alongside her ready for the interview and said: 'Your lipstick's smudged...' She took a sharp intake of breath then I told her I was kidding. I was happy and enjoying myself properly for the first time in a year!

We all shared a whisky with the people who had been there for us the most in the past year.

Vera came over. She had now just about recovered from her bicycle trauma and swore that she would either make every effort to lose several stones in weight or never go back on a bike again! We believed the former was unlikely to the point of impossibility.

Our dear friend Alan, God bless him, shared a whisky conference call with us in Brafferton. It was such a great feeling all day.

I rang my boss at the hospital, Sheenagh. She is also from a farming background and knew what I'd been going through. She'd been great with me at work.

The whole family and what seemed like the whole of our local community then decanted to the Shoulder of Mutton in Kirk Smeaton where the night was long and the atmosphere was extremely merry!

When we got round to reading up the reports we were even more satisfied:

Justice McCombe accused DEFRA of making 'a policy mountain out of what was a farm molehill' by pursuing the case through the courts. Speaking at the High Court in London he told Julie Anderson:

'You made a state trial out of something that could have been dealt with on the farm. This really is a case about one animal.'
Justice McCombe, as reported in Daily Express 15 April 2011

He accused DEFRA of 'defying common sense'.

Our solicitors gave the following statement:

'The judge accepted that DEFRA veterinary surgeons had mishandled the sampling process carried out on the farm and as a consequence did not follow their own guidance specifically designed to prevent contamination and cross-contamination. The Jacksons have always accepted that bovine TB is a disease which should be eradicated from cattle herds if at all possible – but the system adopted for testing has to be consistent and in accordance with published policy and guidelines. In this instance, DEFRA's taking of blood samples failed to comply with its own guidelines, hence the legal challenge and the decision of the High Court which was based not on the opinion of scientists but on what happened in the Yorkshire field the day sampling took place.

'The court heard no evidence to suggest that Hallmark Boxster had bovine TB and the bull had passed a skin test some two weeks before the sampling.

'After an initial injunction postponing the first slaughter notice the judge had suggested that DEFRA should re-test but, for reasons best known to DEFRA that did not happen.'
Barker Gotelee – Solicitors

I know we're wallowing in success here, but grant us this for a moment, because the story was not over just yet. Here are just a few of our favourite headlines from the press:

'BOXY THE BULL ESCAPES THE CHOP OVER TB TEST BUNGLE'
Daily Mail
'JUDGE SLAMS DEFRA AFTER BOXY THE BULL WINS REPRIEVE FROM DEATH SENTENCE'
Yorkshire Post

That wasn't the end of it. We still had a distance to travel in this journey before we were in the clear.

The judge had ruled in our favour. That was indisputable. He had ordered DEFRA to pay us £15,000 towards our legal bills. That too was indisputable. There would be more to come but he had ordered this first amount to be paid in 14 days of his decision. We'd spent far more but were comforted by the fact that more would be ordered to be paid.

But we had won! We had won! We had won!

Chapter 37

Testing Times

DEFRA announced that they had decided not to appeal against Justice McCombe's verdict, which he had warned them not to.

Their reasoning was that 'our immediate priority is to continue to work with the owners of Boxster to resolve the TB problem in their herd.'

What problem? By now we had no reactors on the farm, those suspected of having TB via the various tests the previous year had all been slaughtered and all our subsequent tests had been clear. Boxy's test had been annulled by the judge, yet they were still purporting we had a problem.

Dad told the *Yorkshire Post*:

'I haven't got a TB problem. I have had seven consecutive all-clears, which involved vets walking past Boxster to the rest of the herd and refusing to give him the re-test we asked for in the first place. Officially the 'positive' test on him (last year) is null and void. He is only still in quarantine because I am voluntarily going along with DEFRA's instructions, although they are driving me to the point of explosion.'
Ken Jackson

Animal Health in Leeds had informed us that Boxster would need two clear skin tests and a blood test to be classed as TB free.

We were very concerned for quite a few reasons.

Boxster had already passed a skin test, so we felt all that was needed was a second skin test. That's what the rest of the herd had been judged on.

The herd had been through the skin tests, they were clear, so there was no need for a blood test. Why did the same not apply to Boxster?

The farm was still shut down whilst Boxy's court case had been taking place, but with the judge's ruling being that his blood test was to be discounted surely two successful skin tests would be enough for the whole herd to open up for business properly once again?

Their argument was that every animal on the farm, with the exception of Boxster, had passed the blood test, therefore he needed to as well. Technically speaking we knew they were still in the wrong.

The blood test was only brought into action once you had a reactor through the skin test.

We didn't have any reactors. Our herd was now 100% clear of bovine TB. Our animals had all come through. Boxy had already undergone one successful skin test the previous year. In our eyes that meant when he got through a second skin test we would be back trading as normal.

They were digging in their heels about the blood test.

Another of our concerns was that we now simply didn't trust anyone in DEFRA or Animal Health, with the exception of Avril, with whom we had struck up a friendship.

The rest of them, to us, were the enemy. So far as we were concerned if we never saw any of them again it would be too soon.

We knew that when it came to the skin test we would be able to see the results for ourselves, but we saw DEFRA's intransigence over the blood test as a sign that they had 'issues' with us.

When it comes to a blood sample you are not in control.

They come, they take the blood, cart it off to a laboratory and ring you with the result. That was too many possible loopholes for us.

We believed that DEFRA were now desperate for Boxster's result to come back positive as a reactor. That way they would be able to say they had been right all along.

From an earlier position of innocence and naivety we had become hard-bitten and cynical about DEFRA practice. We were now 'fully-paid-up' members of the conspiracy theory.

Emails we had read during the lead-up to trial from the various DEFRA departments, warning others about the case and sending tip-offs had made us suspicious of everyone.

We felt that a quiet word here or there, no doubt between colleagues who 'owed favours', would be all it would take to undo all the time we had spent. It only needed one person to be in some way aggrieved that we had won, one person who perhaps felt they had a score to settle.

We also knew that if Animal Health had managed to class Boxster as a reactor there might still have been no visible lesions found. And yet they would still say that it wouldn't have meant he hadn't got bovine TB. We would never have been able to prove that he was a negative, but they would have got what we felt they wanted.

This still wasn't over!

Chapter 38

Jim Paice MP

In recognition of the Singing Farmers' efforts for charity, the team received a special award from the RABI in Oxford on 11 May 2011.

One of the reasons they were keen to attend was due to the guest speaker – Jim Paice MP, Minister of State for Agriculture and Food. The boys had spent the evening prior to the event ensuring that they had a plan so that Dad would get some time with Mr Paice to tell him about our blood test issue. Dad had questions ready to ask that we'd prepared at home.

Dad, Chris and Phil (three of the lads) had travelled down together and made sure they were in the right place at the right time for when Mr Paice arrived.

If Dad had expected a level of compassion from a man who had been in farm management and had his own herd of Highland cattle, he was to be bitterly disappointed.

They talked. Dad said that Mr Paice believed that the test had been carried out correctly and that we shouldn't have won. When Dad asked about the testing procedure that Animal Health in Leeds was now trying to force upon us, he told Dad that we should let them get on with it.

Chapter 39

Bring On Edwina

Justice McCombe had recommended that Animal Health decide the best way forward in testing Boxster following his 'null and void' verdict on the 2010 blood test, because they were the experts.

But he had also recommended that no-one should be involved in the arrangements who had previously had an interest. To us that meant someone with no personal feelings about the case, no axes to grind, people who were going to come to it fresh.

That wasn't happening.

Everything was coming from one source and by now you don't need me to tell you who that was.

That's why on 17 May 2011 we refused to deal with the management team at Animal Health in Leeds and insisted that someone else be responsible for whatever was to happen. We hadn't disagreed that some form of testing would take place, we were just mightily suspicious of the intent.

We first spoke with Edwina Thirkell at the end of May.

Edwina was the divisional veterinary manager at Animal Health Leicester. We had a pleasant conversation with her and she said she would also be talking with Peter Gray, her opposite number in Northumberland.

One of the first things we asked was that Boxster be moved to a different isolation pen. His ground was chewed up and as it was now the middle of spring we wanted him to benefit from being in a fresh paddock. She didn't agree instantly but said she'd take a look when she came up. She seemed approachable and we felt positive.

Three days later Edwina and Peter arrived. We were looking on this as a new start with Animal Health, but also with trepidation. They took a look at Boxster's pen and then took a tour of the farm. We talked about the measures that had been put in place to avoid cases of bovine TB in the future.

We went into the house and sat around the table in the main room. Mum and Dad sat to one side of the table, Edwina and Peter to the other, and me at the head. Paul came in and sat on the armchair close by. Edwina gave a formal introduction of who she was, her experience and background. Peter then did the same. She asked Dad, Mum, Paul and me in turn about our lives and what we did.

It was all a little forced, a charade, as though we were in some training session. I wondered where it was going.

After the introductions Edwina got down to the real business of the testing regime. We asked why Boxster needed two skin tests when he'd already passed one in 2010. Why didn't that one count as one of the two?

Edwina told us that because Boxster had come up with a positive blood test he had to go back to square one.

It was yet another clear indication that DEFRA and Animal Health had still not accepted Justice McCombe's ruling.

Once again we tried to get our point across that the judge had ruled it was not a bona fide test. That meant he'd just had one test, a skin test that he'd passed.

Edwina's argument disregarded our comment. She maintained that two skin tests and a blood test were needed. We were going around in circles again.

We weren't over-concerned about the skin tests, whether it was to be one or two, we were still more concerned about the blood test.

That was the one we had no control over once the sample left the farm and in our hearts we still felt that anything could happen to it, regardless of how many new people they sent out to see us, offer platitudes and eat Mum's cakes! We didn't trust them.

Edwina asked what it was about the blood test that concerned us. She asked whether we were scared that the blood test's accuracy would automatically come back as a positive.

We told her what we felt, that the issues of trust, fuelled by the lies in court, were behind it.

This is where we saw the real business edge of this lady.

She had come 'power-dressed', now she was about to wield some of her power. She said that it was ludicrous to think that a government laboratory would tamper with a sample, as we were alluding might happen.

Her next move was to offer to take the sample and deliver it personally to the laboratory.

I declined her offer.

She felt this was a slur on her honesty. All I said was: 'I've only just met you. I don't know you or what you're capable of, or what power you wield in the corridors of where you work.'

She wasn't impressed, but we were serious. What the past year had told us was not to trust anyone in DEFRA. It would take something special for us to put any belief into them.

We moved on to discussing the restrictions on the herd that had still been in place despite getting the all-clear in consecutive tests back in January 2011.

She agreed that the herd restrictions should have been lifted and said she would sign the paperwork there and then. Hallelujah!

The herd was open for business – at least that was one major step forward.

Chapter 40

Blood

By now we had made up our minds there was no way DEFRA were going to listen to our arguments. The only way we were going to get Boxy free again was by having the blood test and two skin tests.

Because we didn't trust DEFRA we considered various options. We weren't concerned about the skin tests as we could see the results first-hand. But the blood test?

We still believed that, whatever was said otherwise, this laid Boxster open to whoever might have wanted to see him fail. Call us paranoid if you like, but if you had been in our position what would you have done?

One of the ideas we discussed was to have three bulls tested, labelling them A, B and C.

At this point someone from the NFU would label them, match them with the ear tag numbers. The laboratory would receive them as purely A, B and C and when the results came back the envelope would be opened to reveal the findings.

Initially we thought this would be a good idea. Then we thought about the blood tests and their accuracy. At 97% accuracy there was always a chance of a false reactor – and by having three bulls tested we would increase our chances of that happening by a further 200 per cent!

We had only just had the herd restrictions lifted. There was just a chance that we would be back to square one.

Peter Gray visited us again. He understood our concerns but stressed that we needed to have the tests done.

On 8 June 2011 Boxster had his first skin test of the two DEFRA required and his blood test.

Jonathan, our vet, conducted the blood test with Peter Gray and a colleague in attendance. We had insisted that the blood test be undertaken before they injected him with bovine TB for the skin test.

Boxy was still in his isolation pen. We hired a portable crush as he couldn't be brought down into the yard. He hadn't been handled for 15 months but you'd never have guessed as he stood calmly. The atmosphere was intense. Nothing was done without everyone seeing. I put nothing on Boxster's tail.

Jonathan struggled a little to get the sample but got it in one go with no loss of vacuum. He inverted the sample eight times in front of us all, counting as he did so. We were then shown the label that was going on the vial and that it corresponded with Boxster's ear tag number.

Perhaps everything was a little over the top, but at least no mistakes were made. The sample was then put into a temperature-controlled box. Jonathan signed a piece of paper on the box, Peter Gray signed too. The lid was put on the box and it was sealed with tape.

By now I was fighting hard to hold back my tears. I watched Boxster's blood sample go and suddenly felt completely out of control. I felt I had personally sealed Boxster's fate by allowing the blood test to happen, that whatever happened from here was my fault. I may as well have signed the slaughter notice myself.

It was as though DEFRA may have had an opportunity to win after all.

Jonathan guided me through the skin test. He showed me the vials of avian and bovine TB. That they were brand new vials. He measured Boxy with his callipers, injected him and Boxster trotted off back into his paddock.

I asked Peter Gray when we would get the results and he said it was being rushed through.

Up until now we were under the impression that this was just a normal test, as with any other animal, treated like any other. Now we were being told it was being 'rushed through'.

It made me even more concerned.

I'd said that the only way we were going to let the sample go was if we went with it, or more accurately if I went with it. But I had been told that this would make no difference, that they do something to the blood as soon as it arrives at the laboratory then store it for 24 hours.

In the hours that followed after his sample left I convinced myself that Boxy was finally destined for slaughter.

Clot

Peter Gray called us on 10 June 2011. He spoke with Paul. It was the only time Paul had ever been called by DEFRA. Boxster's blood sample had clotted and couldn't be processed. It had failed their quality control. What?

How odd was that?

Blood becomes clotted if it is not kept at the correct temperature. Of the previous samples taken from our farm only six out of 118 cattle had needed to be resampled for clotting or any other reason previously.

Boxy's sample had been driven directly there, a special case. Every effort had been made to ensure that it was fresh and had arrived quickly. What were the odds of clotting amongst special cases such as this as opposed to others not dealt with in this way?

Given our now extremely suspicious minds regarding anything that occurred out of the ordinary with DEFRA we were now immediately back on our guard.

When Peter Gray said he had to come out again and re-test Boxster – and that he had already put into place arrangements for doing so – we said no. He asked why.

I told him that having injected him with TB just two days ago he was not coming back and taking another sample on the date he'd suggested.

He tried to explain that the TB which had been injected would be out of his system by then. I told him that the research I had done, and it had been extensive in the lead up to the court case, had told me that experts disagreed with each other.

Some said it could take three days, others said six months. Every animal is different in some way and common sense tells you that not everyone reacts the same.

Did it really clot, or was it not the result DEFRA had wanted?

Either way, we just said this was twice that they had taken blood from our bull and messed it up. How many more times were they going to make mistakes? Was it until they got the result they were after?

Peter Gray's answer was that they would carry on doing it until they got it right. We wondered what getting it right really meant within DEFRA's walls.

We told DEFRA to get stuffed!

Chapter 42

Royal Affair

Boxy passed his first skin test the next day.

This was still under what DEFRA calls its 'severe interpretation' rules. That meant that any lump over two millimetres and Boxster would have been gone! He didn't even show so much as a pimple!

At least one stage of the three was completed.

We were back at the Great Yorkshire Show in July 2011. We had returned to the show ring, minus Boxster of course.

Our return was still sweet though.

Stubbswalden Endeavour was champion bull and reserve champion in the British Blonde junior championship; Violetta was second in the cow class. We also had champion bull in the British Blues with Bentley Brook Dakota.

We had even greater support from what seemed like everyone at the show. The public, many not connected at all to farming, were coming up to us all the time, congratulating us on winning our case.

We had started to receive all kinds of things at home – pictures that people had painted or drawn of Boxy; letters of support; phone calls of well-wishers wanting to come and see him. But our support was about to take on a different dimension at the show.

HRH The Prince of Wales, Prince Charles visited the show on Wednesday 13 July 2011. The previous year when we had written to Prince Charles we had received a letter from his office wishing us well with our endeavours.

We were part of the Grand Parade, which was set to take place that afternoon with Charles and Camilla due to walk around the ring chatting to some of the exhibitors.

Dad had talked with HRH The Queen when she had visited in 2008. I don't suppose that meant we were friends of the family as such, but Dad was up for using any contact he could.

Endeavour had done well, but hadn't taken the overall British Blonde title, so we were about the third Blonde back in the parade. Dad and I were both standing with him when we came to a halt. It's a magnificent spectacle when the parade is all in place.

When we had taken up our place one of the stewards came up to us to say that there needed to be a gap just next to us, because this is where Charles and Camilla were to walk between the cattle. It was like fate, what better position could we have had?

Dad had been saying he was going to get to talk with Charles before we went in the parade, now he was convinced of it.

As they approached us Dad set off walking towards Charles. My first thought was that the security guards were going to dive on him because he was striding so purposely.

They shook hands and had a conversation. Camilla came and talked with me.

Dad's conversation with Charles had been that he didn't know whether he was aware of 'our job with bull'.

Charles had told him he was, but that he had got it all sorted now hadn't he?

Dad said that it wasn't and quickly briefed him on where we had got to. Charles told him that he was due to have a meeting with Rt Hon Caroline Spelman, the Secretary of State for Environment, Food and Rural Affairs (DEFRA) the following day! He said if Dad could get him all the information he would bring it up at the meeting and ask a few questions.

Prince Charles's personal secretary gave us his card – and that was me done for the day!

I spent the rest of the afternoon in the back of the British Blonde Cattle Society tent on my mobile phone producing an email to send. I tried to make it as brief as possible yet still contain all the relevant facts. Alan Hall looked it over for me before I sent it.

We never heard anything from it, but our thought was that if Prince Charles had just made one little mention of it to Caroline Spelman about 'this bloke with the bull' that would have been enough.

Boxy's Freedom

Peter Gray had called us since the 'clotted' blood sample, but we still hadn't agreed to the re-test.

On 18 July 2011 we were issued with an order that stated Boxster had to be re-tested on 19 July or, if not suitable, within the next 14 days. We said that the 19th was not suitable.

We received an email the next day stating that unless we informed Animal Health of a specific date, which had to be a Monday, Tuesday or Wednesday within the next 14 days, that the test would be carried out that day and that Peter Gray was on his way.

If we telephoned or emailed a date in the meantime he would return to base.

We made the call and said we would have the test on Tuesday 2 August 2011 as we had not had time to make any preparations.

Having made the call I then sent the following email to Dermott at Barker Gotelee:

'We would like you to send an official letter to DEFRA asking for an answer to the following: Why do we need to have the gamma test carried out on 2 August, four days before the skin test is due, and not carried out on the same day? (They have calculated the skin test date incorrectly and it is due on 6 August). We have asked the question several times, our vet and the NFU have asked too, but no-one has received an answer that we can understand.'

I had spoken again with Peter Gray and told him that if we

agreed to the blood test being undertaken once again that it was on the same grounds as the previous test, under the same conditions. That meant taking the blood sample first then injecting Boxster for the skin test afterwards on the same day.

At first Peter Gray refused on the basis that their protocol – here we go again – stated that they needed the results of the blood test prior to the skin test result.

At this point I told Peter that he had said the results of the blood test could be 'rushed through' in three days, as he had said with the 'clotted' test. The skin test is undertaken in three days. What was their problem?

Policy, policy, policy – that seems as though it is DEFRA's mantra, not let's all work together as Dad says we should.

Eventually they saw sense and decided to do it our way.

Later that week Animal Health agreed that both tests would be carried out at the same time with the blood sample being taken prior to the TB injections. The date was arranged for Tuesday 9 August with Avril and Peter Gray attending.

But I had another dilemma.

I wasn't going to be there for it. Andrew and I were due to be away on holiday and we couldn't delay the test any further.

Before I went away I had put arrangements in place. I arranged for a good friend of mine, a veterinary nurse, Alex Clifton, to oversee what happened.

I gave her strict instructions. Another of my closest friends, Ellen, was there too. I asked her to take notes about anything and everything that took place. The evening before the test, whilst I was on holiday, they both emailed me to pack it in.

The day of the test was Andrew's birthday. It seemed as though main events in Boxster's past year and a half had always happened on family birthdays. It had been mine when we had the first reactor; and Mum's when he had tested 'positive'.

Alex sent me a message telling me both tests had been completed and the sample had gone. What came as a surprise was that Ellen and Dad had gone with it. This hadn't been a part of my plans.

What had happened?

'I said that the sample wasn't going anywhere without me. We went with Peter to Stratford upon Avon. We handed it over to the laboratory technician in charge. I asked whether there was anything I could watch him do to give me confidence that it would be handled properly.'
Ken Jackson

Dad and Ellen had waited for the sample to be taken and then told Peter Gray they wanted to accompany it.

Peter was taking it straight to the laboratory and said he didn't know whether he could get them back home if they went with him.

They said they could catch a train. He agreed they could go. At least we knew it had got there without being tampered. But now we were back in limbo, in the hands of DEFRA's laboratory until Friday.

I was still away on holiday when the result was due. It came a day early and had come in an email from Peter Gray.

It read 'Good news'. I couldn't download the full message. I started smacking my phone, telling Andrew that I thought Boxster had passed his blood test.

He calmly took the phone from me and told me I had another email from Mum. She had sent one saying he'd passed!

'I just felt justice had been done. Peter Gray had said that he was really pleased for us. He was a decent man doing a difficult job. I emailed Kate then went to find Ken. When I found him, we stood there and held each other in the middle of the yard.'
Anita Jackson

They were all drinking whisky back at home. I was in the Mediterranean, which was lovely, but right then I just felt I should have been there drinking with them.

They were ecstatic.

We still had the skin test result to come the following day, but this had been our biggest worry. I had now moved on to worrying about tomorrow's test.

'Have you been looking at him closely to check for any lump?' Dad was telling me not to worry.

This was the last hurdle. Alex and Ellen were both coming back for the result the following day.

Avril conducted the test with Peter Gray present. She had brought a bottle of champagne with her but had kept it in her car until she had completed the test.

She said she hadn't dared get it out of the car beforehand just in case.

Boxy was completely in the clear, no lump present at all.

Boxster was free!!!

Chapter 44

The Release

But before we put Boxy back in with the herd, which we could have done there and then, there was something else to consider. There always seemed to be something!

The herd was due its six-month test just after I was back from holiday.

Because we had suffered positive reactors previously we were now on a six-month testing regime rather than four-yearly.

We decided that to put him back in the herd prior to the herd test would expose him to testing once again, so reluctantly we decided to leave him in his isolation pen for a while longer. Once the whole herd passed, as they had several times by now, we would then let him return to the fold.

Avril came back once again. She injected them all. Three days later she was back.

This was what football managers now call 'squeaky bum' time. We were all holding our breath as every animal went through.

One by one they went through with no problem. I think it's the most Paul and I have ever looked at each other. You could see the concern in his eyes, and I'm sure he saw it in mine.

There were another seven to go through. Those last seven were an agonising time.

The last animal went through. I opened the crush with tears rolling down my face. Mum was the same.

Dad picked up Avril and gave her a hug.

And Paul went, 'Woah!'

The herd was clear, Boxy was already clear. He could finally return to the rest of the herd. We didn't need telling twice. He was on his way!

The *Yorkshire Post*, who had been brilliant throughout, sent a photographer.

By the time he arrived we had Boxy out of his isolation pen, I was brushing him, preparing him for what was the big day we had been looking forward to.

Once the photographer had taken the really cheesy shots with me cuddling up close to Boxy, which I actually really liked, he took up position for us to release him into the field with the rest of the herd.

Dad let the cows out from their pens and they all came streaming across the yard into the field. Dad took off Boxy's nose ring clip and Boxy walked forward towards the cows.

He moved cautiously. Then he looked back at Dad as if to say, 'Is this alright? Do you know I'm stood in the middle of all these cows? All these females?'

Within seconds you could see his expression change and he set off trotting down the lane with the cows. The minute he got into the open field he galloped, skipped and bucked just like a pony.

Then he set off for another gallop and the rest of the herd galloped with him.

Chapter 45

The Original Conclusion – Updated

When this book was first written in 2012, we said it would be very unlikely Boxy would ever see a show ring again. He was robbed of what could have been a majestic second season.

We had looked forward to showing him after his glorious success in 2009. As long as he continued walking well and looked well, he would have been competing in 2010, 2011 and even 2012.

He had been denied what should have been his halcyon period due to intransigence from a government department, from an organisation that a High Court judge ended up ruling against.

Our challenge had never been about money, but if we had lost I would have felt terrible for Mum, Dad, Paul and his family.

Boxy's value, not our valuation, was £20,000. Our costs reached £126,000. DEFRA were ordered to pay us £120,000. They offered £80,000. We were advised to settle at £90,000.

It's not exactly a brilliant profit and loss account is it? As Dad said, we would never have been able to take this on at all if we had been tenant farmers. It would have been far too much risk.

But Boxy was still with us and we had that personal satisfaction of knowing that all our efforts had been vindicated.

We thanked and still thank everyone who helped or supported us during those months – and we hoped most sincerely and still do that others never have to go through it, but that should anyone suffer the way we had, we hoped this book would help in some way.

So, now let's tell you what happened next and how 'Boxy the Bull that never died' lived on and still lives on in our hearts today!

Chapter 46

Boxy & His Girls

I cannot begin to describe how it felt, seeing Boxy getting turned out with the cows, his girls. It still makes me emotional now.

He'd been so miserable. He'd been isolated for so long and I didn't really know how he would react.

I guess he couldn't understand why his life had changed. If it had been me in a similar position where I had been quarantined but nobody had been able to tell me why, I would have thought what the hell's wrong? What have I done? What's going on?

Boxy hadn't seen another cow for 17 months! He was one fit, magnificent, champion bull and bulls aren't fit and magnificent for nothing! He was in his prime. He should have been doing what bulls do!

He really couldn't see the cows because he was well away from them and around a corner. I'm sure he could hear them – and that must have been torture!

Boxy was nearly three and a half years old when his isolation started. The breeding ability of bulls is usually at its peak at around 36 months and it will normally start declining in performance at between five and six years of age. He was now coming up to five years old when he was released.

All of that natural maturity and testosterone was there and had been there for some time and I cannot imagine what it must have been like for him. All charged up and ready to perform but with no performance allowed.

It still amazes me that he didn't turn nasty in any way at all. No animal-to-animal contact, no animal-to-human contact.

He really was in complete isolation since we had removed Katie from the field in April 2010. It was now August 2011.

We hadn't been allowed in the field to see him. I'd been misty-eyed with tears by the gate so many times.

Boxy must have been so sexually frustrated. All of his hormones were probably telling him that he should have been putting himself to better use than tramping around his isolation pen. We couldn't even take semen from him, which you do with bulls that you believe others will buy. It just wasn't allowed while he was quarantined. That might have at least been some form of stress relief.

What Boxy had endured is referred to as a compromised welfare state. Often that is attributed to poor animal husbandry on behalf of the owners.

We did all we could for him within the strictures put on us by Animal Health, who you would think, given their title, would be in favour of an uncompromised welfare state! I will never forgive them for the damage they could have done to Boxy's mind. I still don't know how, after all that time in isolation, he managed to come out of that situation, be led on a rope again after such a long time, and still be my loveable Boxy!

And I needn't have worried about his prowess and performance capability! He certainly hadn't lost it!

Boxy knew exactly his role and he was straight back on the job! As he ran around the field with the cows it was as though he was greeting each one, but he wasn't sniffing them, he was nuzzling! He really was a charmer!

There was such excitement in the field that day. There were about 30 cows and heifers all receiving Boxy's welcome. And the calves loved it too, they were all running, bucking and skipping. It really was a wonderful time!

I'm sure he soon forgot about me! He had his ladies to see, at long last!

He was back where he belonged, and his life went back to normal. A proper bull's life grazing the fields and satisfying his harem.

Dad has grazing land at the village of Womersley and he'd often be there. I'd go and see him regularly and I knew that for all the attention he was giving his girls he hadn't forgotten about me at all.

There's a bit of a hill at Womersley and if I went and shouted for Boxy he would fly down it towards me, sometimes to the point where I would think, 'Oh My God, he's not going to stop!' It was quite scary when he did this. He didn't seem to be slowing down and this was some size bull to be travelling at that pace. If any impact had been made, I probably wouldn't be here now, no matter how wonderful a bull!

Chapter 47

We Decided to Write a Book

Shortly after Boxy's release we called Chris (Berry) to ask him to write what became *Boxster's Story: The Truth Behind the Bull*, the book you've already now read from chapter 2 to 45 and the brand new chapters from Chapter 46 onwards.

Chris had been involved in writing about Boxy's case in the *Yorkshire Post* and he had encouraged Dad to talk about Boxy during the Singing Farmers Concerts. Chris had just completed a book and has written many more. He was available to write *Boxster's Story* and we began the interviews.

'I'd known Ken, Anita, Paul, Kate and Andrew for a number of years through writing stories about their farm and their cattle, seeing them regularly at shows and the attachment Ken and I had as being part of the Singing Farmers. Ken had won a Farming Personality of the Year award in 2003 through a magazine I published called Farming in Yorkshire *just before we had started our concerts.*

'I remember visiting Forlorn Hope with the previous year's winner Phillip Holden who also became one of the Singing Farmers and Ken serenading us in the farmyard.

'I'd followed the whole of Boxy's and the family's plight in 2010 and 2011, after having also witnessed his all-conquering show season year of 2009. He truly was a formidable, outstanding bull. You didn't have to be a livestock man or woman to understand.

'I'd seen this young, pretty, feisty and competitive cattle handler many times over the years, and had probably seen her grow up around the show rings – and I'd talked with Ken and photographed

him with winning beasts for several years.

'Ken is such a sociable bloke, likes a pint and a natter, and a whisky. We had become even greater friends when he and Kate and others from the Blonde Society took part in Housewives Choice, a competition I'd organised for the Great Yorkshire Show that brings members of the public into the ring to judge what they believe is the best breed at the show. Ken loved this because the rules were there were no rules – and I encouraged the handlers to chat-up the ladies!

'We then became even firmer friends through the Singing Farmers. I was delighted when I was asked by Ken and Kate to write Boxster's Story as I have been again to write Boxy.

'Right at the start I knew this would be an emotional rollercoaster for Kate and Anita as they would have to relive their experiences. The whole family had gone through hell and I knew they wanted to vent their spleen over how they had felt treated by DEFRA and to share their experiences with other farmers.'

Chris Berry

We started working on the book in the autumn of 2011 and it was launched with an open day at the farm on 30 June 2012.

But even then, so much happened between Boxy being released and the book coming out. We lost Alan (Hall) on 5 February 2012, Boxy had more tests, my fibromyalgia kicked in harder than ever and my boss left where I had been working in the simulation centre in the hospital.

Dad had dedicated the first book to Alan. He'd been a constant source of encouragement throughout, a fabulous help at shows for years and but for his questioning of the vials and contamination issues when we were preparing for the meeting at Selby Livestock Market we may have never won in the High Court.

Alan's passing was a massive loss to Mum and Dad. He was a true friend and always had a smile on his face.

Boxy wasn't getting away from the testing game. He'd had another six-month test after release, but he'd sailed through. Life back on the farm started returning to normal for Dad, Paul and Mum.

My own work was quite a different matter. The hospital was my job and I was happy being involved in it.

Sheenagh had been my boss. She'd been great while all of our Boxy stuff was going on. She was from a farming background. Sheenagh had appreciated what I was going through and had also been supportive when my fibromyalgia had kicked in, which it had done during the times we were tackling the case and it had become even worse after the case had finished.

It's like when you end with the stress of something, that's when other things hit you. It seems your adrenaline can keep you going while you're fighting but then when you can't keep it up or when the fight is over and you start to relax, you're vulnerable. That's what happened to me – and sometimes, as I now see it, there are people who take advantage of your weakness.

While Sheenagh was my direct boss above me, above Sheenagh were the two Alistairs and here, once again, I'd had support from one of the Alistairs who told me he'd been anticipating this happening. What he meant was he'd expected me to plummet at some stage given my condition and the circumstances he knew we'd been involved with on the farm. The way Alistair put it was, 'You keep fighting and then all of a sudden you can't.'

He was right. I became quite poorly and while Boxy was out doing his thing, flexing his muscles in every area, I was losing all of my muscle strength. It was really hard. I was still doing my job but I'd do a day at work and then have to spend the next day in bed. I went part-time. Sheenagh understood and rostered my role one day on, one day off.

Sharon, who I worked with for a number of years, always helped me out if my fibro became too bad by say three in the afternoon. She would discreetly step in if she could see I was struggling on certain days.

Good news for Sheenagh but bad news for me was that she was promoted and moved on. My new boss was to be a girl I had trained up. This part was seriously not a problem. It was fine. She had a degree and wanted the job. I wasn't bothered she'd been given it. It wasn't something I would have wanted. I liked being on the shop floor, throwing myself down, pretending to be ill or having a fit or whatever role-play was called for.

What happened next, I cannot go into great detail here suffice to say that life became extremely difficult for me under the new post-Sheenagh regime. A good friend of mine who worked in HR for a big company told me to be very careful. She said, 'Trust me, I know exactly where this is going,' and advised me to delete any email that wasn't a work email and empty my locker of anything personal.

Initially I told her to stop being daft, but I then did as she said. Again, I won't go into everything here but I felt they had 'done a number on me' and just wanted rid of me.

They pulled me out of a session I was running and made several points, all of which I challenged, but I was heartbroken.

When I left work the day I had been humiliated I was in shock and devastated. I went to Mum and Dad's to pick up Patrick and Gemma. I cried my eyes out. I'd rung Andrew and he came straight away.

To make this part as short as possible my HR friend Sarah helped me through this period, as did several others. I almost appeared in court again, their own court in London, but I fought them for about a year on unpaid leave. Having done my evidence-gathering bit again and having submitted a 94-page document and having attended a hearing or two, as they postponed one, an agreement was reached and I was offered my position back.

I politely turned them down. It was a great feeling. I left work officially in October 2012.

But while all these shenanigans were going on we were writing the book. Chris, me, Mum, Dad and Paul were all involved. In some ways it was hard reliving it all, but it was also cathartic. We were getting it all down.

Over 400 turned up for the book launch and fittingly a couple of days earlier Boxy finally had his first-born calf! We ran a competition to name it and Hallmark Hallelujah was the winning entry from a lady who has turned out to be my dearest friend (after Andrew, of course!). Sue Wilson of Burnt Yates, who has her own herd.

Sue had bought a bull from Dad years before and had followed Boxy's story. Sue has become my sounding board, someone I can tell every hairbrained idea and scheme I come up with and she listens. We talk every day and I see her, in non-Covid times, as often as I can. It's such a friendship and Sue is definitely one of the best things to have happened to me since those days.

The open day was fantastic. There was so much love and happiness around. It was a magical time after all we had gone through previously. Everyone was smiling. Life was good!

Chapter 48

My Own Little Herd

I had no idea that what we had gone through with Boxy in 2010 and 2011 would lead to such amazing years ahead – and everything Andrew and I experienced in the show rings, particularly over a fantastic three-year period from 2015-2017 is all directly attributable to Boxy. And there was far more! This bull that lived on was the inspiration for everything.

When I finally called it quits at work, having dealt with those who I felt wanted me out in a similar way to how I'd dealt with DEFRA, I took on three heifers from Dad. This wasn't about anything more than providing me with some exercise in an environment I loved, back on the farm at Forlorn Hope. Andrew and I only lived about a mile away. It was ideal. Fortunately, Andrew's business was going well. We were in a decent position financially.

I had been having physio through hydrotherapy to allow my muscle strength to build back up again following the effects of fibromyalgia and buying the heifers from Dad was more physio. It was perfect for me as it meant I had to do jobs like carrying buckets and feeding the heifers, but if for whatever reason I couldn't then Dad or Melvin were there to help.

Fibromyalgia is triggered by stress, either physical or mental, and the anxiety we had had during Boxy's horrible two years, followed by the year I'd endured by certain people at work was, in retrospect, always going to take its toll sometime.

Being back on the farm and being able to concentrate on something good and positive once again, was my therapy. It gave me rehab. I now had three heifers of my own to look after – Fern, Ellie 'Big Belly' and Gemma. It was a happy time after all of the emotional stress I'd been under and the physical problems this had brought on.

Andrew would come on his way home from work and help me with the girls. Andrew has always been there for me, every step of the way, and now he was starting to get more involved with the cattle too.

The other thing was that I was still with Boxy!

Dad had a lot of young bulls around, so we had plenty of choice for putting our heifers in calf, but it was just a given what was going to happen! I don't recall ever asking Dad whether I could use Boxy, I just 'borrowed' him. Our little herd was about to grow!

What we didn't know at that time was that it was to include a cow that, combined with Boxy, would set Andrew and I on other amazing adventures that would see us achieve so much personally and in the show rings once again, but now under our own herd prefix. Even then, though, it came out of sadness elsewhere.

Alan's passing in February of 2012 had left his wife Carol with a herd of cattle that needed looking after. Carol was in bad health and it was too much for her. Seeing them in the yard at Brafferton must have been a constant reminder of Alan at a time when she wasn't very well at all. I'd become much closer with Carol since he'd passed. We'd spent a lot of time together.

Carol had someone helping her look after the herd of about 20 cattle, but coping was still difficult. She rang Dad and asked him over to take them to Forlorn Hope, value them and sell them. We all went up in a convoy and brought them back.

One of the problems Carol had had since Alan's passing had been that she couldn't get any of the cows back in calf. It was like they were traumatised at Alan not being around. I swear to this day that the cows were in mourning of his passing. He'd spent a lot of time with them and they were or had become a man's animal. They did not like women!

When I went in with them back at Forlorn Hope none of them would entertain me, but they would make a right old fuss with Dad and I think he helped them get over the loss of Alan.

After Dad had valued the herd Carol asked whether he would pay the valuation he'd put on. She didn't want them to be sold at a sale in a livestock market, she wanted them to stay where they would be cared for and so Dad said, 'Yeah.'

Alan had one very special animal. His pride and joy was a cow that he'd bought in Borderway livestock market in Carlisle when she was an in-calf heifer. He'd spent a lot of money to get her, he'd shown her and she, like Boxy, was unbeaten. This was Ark Dora.

Dora was a bit like Carol, feisty but lovable. Carol hated her. She said Dora was a bitch! Dora would go for Carol any time she went near her, but because Dora's value was a lot higher than the other animals in the herd she had decided to put her up for sale via sealed bids.

I wouldn't have even been thinking about bidding for Dora when she first arrived at Forlorn Hope because Carol was right. Dora was a bitch! Every time I went near her pen she'd come running and try to headbutt me! I'd slap her and tell her off. This went on for weeks, but we got to the stage where she would let me stroke her and we developed such a relationship that I fell in love with her.

I didn't want Dora going to anyone she didn't mean anything to – and by now I really wanted her for my little herd. She was such a special animal.

Andrew and I stretched ourselves financially to make what we hoped would be the winning bid. I rang Carol to tell her we were putting in all that we could afford, but not to be offended if she felt it was not enough for her and also not to feel in any way obliged because of our friendship or our family's friendship.

On the closing date in 2013 Carol rang and said, 'She's yours!' Tragically Carol passed away a year later on 19 May 2014, just before Andrew and I began our show career together.

Dora took my herd to four, joining the other three girls.

Boxy went and did his stuff with Dora and the year their first calf, a heifer calf, was born the initial letter for all pedigree calves was J. I named her Justice, because after all that had happened, she was my justice.

We showed Dora with Justice as a calf at foot in 2014 – and that's when a new name in the showing world was born!

But before all that happened we had yet another fright with Boxy!

Chapter 49

Boxy's Magic Powder

It was the second summer following his release and it must have happened overnight.

I went into the field to have my usual morning cuddle with Boxy, but when he got up he couldn't put any load-bearing weight on his right rear leg and was quickly lifting it back up again. It gave the effect of his leg swinging.

Jonathan of Bishopton Vets was back again. After I had led Boxy towards him and then away Jonathan broke the bad news.

When a bull angles itself to bull a cow, his disc can slip. It is very rare but can happen.

Boxy had slipped a disc that was pressing on his spinal cord. When you looked along his back you could see that where his hips would be, there was a big dip. You could see where it had gone.

There was nothing we could do. Jonathan said he couldn't walk properly as he had no feeling in his leg, the slipped disc was causing him pain and that it wouldn't get any better. He would get worse over time. He would become paralysed.

Jonathan suggested that the only thing we could do, because of his prowess, would be to take semen from him.

After all we had been through less than two years ago this was another massive blow and maybe the final blow. As you can imagine my emotions were really high. My tears started all over again. Mum and Dad were emotional too. There was whisky, surprise, surprise!

Jonathan mentioned that from a pain point of view Boxy

would be fine while the semen was taken, but that we would have to apply for a licence to do so – and that would mean he would have to have a series of tests. One of which would be a bovine TB test!

By this time, since the win in the High Court, Boxy had flown through every test, but I always had in mind we were exposing him to DEFRA's clutches. I'd always felt they would have him at the slightest opportunity and here we were giving Animal Health another go!

We made the decision to take semen from Boxy and we applied for the licence. Bishopton Vets came out, conducted all the tests and Boxy passed every single one.

But he wasn't a happy bull. He spent much of his time laid down to avoid the pain. He was already effectively paralysed.

I had to do something. Anything. This was my Boxy. The bull that never dies!

We were working with a local feed company owner, Stuart Cornforth, trialling a newly designed feed on Dora and Justice. It has since become available on the market.

Stuart told me about a powder he was also working on called Goldform, which he said was all herbal, based around turmeric which helps with arthritis and a natural anti-inflammatory. At the time it was unlicenced, and he didn't know what it would do for Boxy, but said we could give it a try.

I was prepared to give anything a try! Stuart started supplying the powder and I was mixing it with his feed for him morning and night, while also massaging the muscles around his slipped disc where it was rock hard. He would occasionally go into spasms. I was undertaking physiotherapy for cattle.

Weeks later, Jonathan came with his kit to take Boxy's semen one day and could not believe his eyes when he saw Andrew and me power-washing a now upright bull stood immaculately on four legs. He didn't realise it was Boxy, because he hadn't anticipated seeing him up and about. He said something along the lines of:

'What the bloody hell have you done to him? How have you

got him to this?'

I told him about what we now called 'Boxy's Magic Powder'.

Jonathan said: 'Whatever you're doing, keep doing it. I can't believe the difference in him.'

Boxy wasn't back with the cows but he could certainly walk a lot better. Jonathan took two lots of semen from him. Boxy stood in the crush for about an hour and a half and walked straight back out as though it was all the most natural thing in the world!

I said to Jonathan: 'Do you think he will be able to work again?'

Jonathan said: 'Work? I didn't think he'd be able to walk again, let alone work. For the small number of cows he'll be working on with yours, let him. That's what he's for and it's what he should be doing. At least if he slips it again you'll know he's gone happy!'

They were our thoughts too! He went back to work – and had his magic powder every day!

Chapter 50

The Katem Herd

Every pedigree breeder has a herd name, but we didn't have one just prior to showing Dora in 2014. She was in the trailer as we left Mum and Dad's bound for the Lincolnshire Show. We were pulling onto the A1 and trying to come up with a herd name.

A lorry went past. The name of the haulage company was Katem. Andrew and I both thought, that works! Kate McNeil – Katem was born! You could say, as I did at the time, that we had nicked it off the back of a lorry!

Dora had a fantastic show season, but the following three years were to be even more successful!

Katem Jewel was born in January 2014 and was out of Fern from my herd and sired by Dad's bull Stubbswalden Geordieboy. Most importantly she was also a Hallmark Boxster granddaughter!

In 2015 she repeated Boxy's feat of being champion at every show she attended including Supreme Champion Blonde at the Great Yorkshire Show!

She wiped the board at the Great Yorkshire, winning as Junior Champion, Female Champion and then the Breed Champion. She was only 18 months old and was up against much more mature animals. It takes a brave judge to give it to an animal of that age, putting it above seniors, particularly at a show of that calibre.

Eric Mutch of Banff in Scotland, the judge, said that she was a 'near perfect heifer' and Andrew said, 'Why, what's wrong with her?'

Eric then just laughed and shook his head. I think he appreciated Andrew's humour.

Justice didn't do as well as Jewel, but no other animal did anyway!

We'd shown both of them that year and Jewel was Andrew's! He just said she could do no wrong and called her 'Mi Julie' after the Ali G song. Andrew and I still argue over whose was the best that year.

Meanwhile, back at Forlorn Hope, Boxy was still officially in Dad's herd. I would borrow him when my ladies were ready and there was a point when we just moved him across the yard into my pen one day and he never moved back to Dad's pen!

By now we were starting to run out of space for the cattle at Forlorn Hope. Ours had all had calves and they were all growing up. They were all either back in calf or had given birth again. Our numbers were quickly increasing, and we were getting in the way. We talked about putting up new buildings at Dad's, but the idea of having our own place was to come next.

Andrew was reorganising his business at the time and sold a part of it which would have allowed us to invest in either a new building on the farm or try to find our own place where the Katem herd could grow. I think you know where this is going don't you?

The Katem herd was to have its own home. We were on the move!

Wrancarr Mill

'Oh my God, you're Boxster's mum!'

This was the moment that set the ball rolling for our move to Wrancarr Mill in the village of Trumfleet. It's about six and a half miles from Forlorn Hope.

We'd looked at quite a few properties, we'd attended a few auctions and had missed out on places. Each time we'd been heartbroken.

We'd seen Wrancarr Mill advertised but there had been something about it that had never made us arrange a viewing. We drove around to it one day, stopped at the end of the lane leading to the property and we were still unsure but decided that we would at least take a look.

It had been a stud farm for horses. There was nothing wrong with it having been that way, but we were still far from convinced that it was for us. We were on our way back home, another dud.

We were getting in the car when Amanda, the owner, said: 'I recognise you.' We went through possible links such as my hospital career. Amanda was a nurse in a local prison.

Andrew mentioned Boxy and that's when Amanda said the opening line to this chapter.

Boxy again!

It is as though everything we've done since his big show year of 2009 and then what happened with Animal Health in 2010 and 2011 has nearly all been inspired by this wonderful bull.

Amanda said that she had followed his story. Suddenly we had a link and she was so interested in him that I said if she ever wanted to come and see him it would be no problem, that he loved seeing people.

By now we had been renting a field opposite our house in Stubbs Walden. Our cattle were grazing. Amanda came, met Boxy, gave him a cuddle, we had a chat over coffee and a few days later she rang to thank me.

We'd just had a cow abort at seven months pregnant, Gemma. When we'd had her tested the result had come back that she'd had neospora. It's a parasite that comes from dog faeces and is an infectious cause of abortion in cows that are in-calf. There was a public footpath which ran through the field.

The infection put the rest of the herd at risk if they had continued to graze the contaminated grass and once they had all been tested for neospora it proved another devastating blow as we lost four breeding females of our eight at the time.

Amanda had rung just as we had found out and I was a bit panicked by it all as we had nowhere else to put them. Dad didn't have any grazing available at the time. We didn't have the funds to pay for rent over and above what we were already paying for the field that was now useless to us.

When Amanda found out our situation, she was there for us like a shot.

She said: 'Bring them here and I'll look after them. They can graze for free.' It was so kind of Amanda. And that's what we did with the girls we had left and Boxy. Andrew and I came every day.

Jewel and Justice stayed at Forlorn Hope as the show animals weren't out grazing.

Amanda was great with the cattle and every time Andrew and I came we'd have a chat and a cuppa in the house. It became familiar and we were comfortable around the farm. We already had our own places around the kitchen table and still sit in them today. We fell in love with Wrancarr Mill.

As we realised this was the place we wanted and things started to get real, Andrew sat me down one night and laid it all on the line what we were actually doing and his concerns.

Andrew asked me whether I could do it, because of my fibromyalgia. He said that he needed to know that I could get up and feed the animals, be there for them. It wasn't an ultimatum, but he was concerned. He said he would always be here to help, but I could totally understand where he was coming from. He had his own business to run too.

He knew I wanted to do all of this, but he also knew that wanting and being physically able to do it are two very different things.

I knew that when I had bad days I physically would not be able to do anything, let alone get out of bed! I couldn't promise him that I would be able to do everything every day because I didn't know. One day I would be fine, next day not.

So, it was a really big risk in some respects, particularly for Andrew as he would have to cover for any time I couldn't, as well as maintain his own business. And we were spending an awful lot of our earnings on this gamble that I was going to be able to cope.

But what drove me was Boxy. Sure, we had our own herd but I wanted him with me, with us. I knew he'd be alright with Dad's animals, but I also knew that I wouldn't see him all the time. Dad would stroke him and loved him but I still felt that nobody else could care for him like I would, spending often nearly half an hour giving him a cuddle each morning.

After that talk we moved heaven and earth to buy Wrancarr Mill.

In short, we needed to sell our place in Stubbs Walden before we could buy anything else, we had another house that we rent out so that brings another income and we had finance from Andrew's sale of a business.

We knew we wouldn't qualify for a mortgage because the new business Andrew had started needed three years of trading. We had to sell where we lived, but it was taking time.

Amanda wanted to sell to people who would love it and we already did! But she knew it had to be sold come what may. We'd looked at bridging loans and remortgaging. We had become excited when the agricultural side of a bank reckoned they would back it, but that fell through.

We finally managed to sell our property and put our offer in just the day before a cash buyer who was looking to stay in the area and who had horses was due to view Wrancarr Mill. It would have been ideal for her, but Amanda accepted our offer and we were in!

Without Boxy we wouldn't be here now, because Amanda wouldn't have mentioned that she felt she knew me – and she wouldn't have known me other than through Boxy. That bull has got a lot to answer for!

We moved here in March 2016 and Boxy was loaded into the trailer and brought here, after having wintered back at Forlorn Hope. I don't even think I ever had a conversation about Boxy becoming mine with Mum and Dad, it was just assumed. Boxy officially became part of the Katem herd.

Boxy was mine! Not that this had ever been in doubt!

Chapter 52

Three in a Row

Having Boxy and Dora together was a fantastic combination. Sometimes you can have a really good bull and a really good cow but that doesn't necessarily mean they're going to produce something special. It just depends on whether they click – and they did!

Boxy was due to be ten years old in October 2016 and Dora was eight years old. Justice had exceeded all breed averages from being born and was in the show team again in 2016. Boxy and Dora had produced again, and we had high hopes.

We had also, by then and before moving to Wrancarr Mill, purchased two more cracking heifers from renowned Blonde breeder Alan Keith in Seaton Burn, near Newcastle upon Tyne – Ark Hermione and Ark Harmony.

Ark Hermione was full sister to Ark Dora, who Alan and Carol Hall had purchased from Alan Keith in 2009.

We were fully committed to showing under our own herd name and building a reputation. During the period of 2015 to 2017 we succeeded probably more so than we had ever imagined.

Jewel's great year of 2015 was followed by other fabulous results for Le Kracker, a Boxster grandson out of Fern. He was Junior and Male Blonde breed champion at both the Great Yorkshire Show and Lincolnshire Show in 2016; and McAlan – after Alan (Hall), not the whisky! – another winner for the Boxster/Dora combination, who also took the Junior champion title at the Great Yorkshire Show in 2017.

That meant we'd completed a successive hat-trick of Junior

champions at the Great Yorkshire Show and all of them bred by you know who! Yep, Boxy!

And that wasn't all by any stretch of the imagination! During this three-year period, we were attending the summer agricultural shows nearly every weekend.

Andrew and I made a point of looking professional, our own Katem livery for ourselves and our cattle. We had a green and gold theme. Everything matched – what we were wearing, our halters, buckets, the lot.

I needed people to associate me with my own herd and be recognised as separate from Dad. There was never any bad feeling. Mum and Dad have always understood.

I'm still Kate Jackson, Ken's daughter to so many people, rather than Kate McNeil with the Katem herd – although that's a nice thing, it is also why we spent time building up the name.

Three successive junior champions, female and male champions and a Supreme breed champion at the Great Yorkshire Show was one hell of a start!

You never know quite what's around the corner whether you're a Jackson or McNeil, but for the Katem herd 2017 proved to be the end or at the very least a long pause to the showing of our herd.

And in the meantime, between the end of the show season of 2017 and the start of the 2018 season, there was something that had to be done, something I didn't want to have done.

I hope you're ready for this next bit.

Chapter 53

Goodbye Boxy

Boxy would struggle each winter, taking time to get up. He was getting older and time catches up on us all. He was still having his magic powder and I was still giving him my bull version of physiotherapy, but I was always worried about him and it became more and more obvious that he was finding life difficult.

But then spring would hit, the weather would change, we would turn him out and he would roll around in the field! I remember saying, 'Don't roll!' as I was worried that he would slip his disc again, while also enjoying the fact that he was having fun. He was fine back out in the field. As long as he was out, up and having his magic powder he was fine.

I wanted him to live forever and if I could have had him in the house with me I would have done!

Andrew worried about me and how I would cope if one day I would go out to the shed and Boxy really wouldn't be able to get up at all. He started talking with me about how we should plan to let him go and to make sure it was handled by the people I wanted involved. I'll let Andrew take over here for a bit, while I get a tissue:

'Having her own cattle was something Kate had always wanted and Boxster was a big part of her life. When we came to Wrancarr Mill, Kate wanted Boxy to come and do a job for us, as well as it being a bit of a retirement home for him.

'We always knew there was going to come a time when we would have to prepare for Boxy not being around.

'When it came to the winter of 2017-2018, his age and ailments, including arthritis, caught up with him. We called upon the people we knew the most to handle it all for us. They were people who understood.'

Andrew McNeil

Every time we brought up the idea of planning for saying goodbye to Boxy I would have tears streaming down my face. I loved this animal so much and we had been through so many things together. This was something I knew needed to happen, but I desperately didn't want it to either.

I don't really know what made me decide. It was around the end of November 2017. We had been in Leeds shopping. We had taken Andrew's car for a service and as we were walking back to the garage I think Andrew began broaching it once again, probably on the basis that I was less likely to cry in public. He knows, you know!

Because I'd made the decision that we had to do it I rang Jonathan at Bishopton while we were walking down the road in Leeds. It was time.

I wanted to have Boxy buried here at Wrancarr Mill. Jonathan then said you had to apply for permission to bury a bovine animal from you know who … DEFRA!!! That there were many regulations. Would Boxy's burial even be granted?

I said to Andrew that we should just do it ourselves and find a way of getting round the system somehow.

Andrew said: 'Absolutely NOT!' That it would only take one person to see us digging a big hole and we could be in big trouble. We have always been honest and we weren't about to change that.

He also said how was I expecting to put Boxy in it without anyone seeing? I was thinking all sorts.

Andrew has always anchored me, and he did so again by saying that I couldn't do something like that anyway, to Boxy. He said I couldn't watch him being lowered into a grave, that it all needed to be done with dignity.

Typically for me, before Andrew said this, I was thinking about getting a petition up, getting public support for a burial, but then Andrew came up with an even more convincing argument that, 'We're not going to live here forever. What happens when we move?' And that was it. I thought hmmm. It's right. We couldn't then dig him up and take him with us!

I know this all sounds like crazy, mad woman territory, but I look at it like this. I loved Boxy so much and we had such a bond that I didn't want to be without him whatever happened. I'd committed myself to the fact he wasn't going to be around, but I was struggling with the 'how' side of things.

Hold on to your hats on the next thought! Taxidermy!

Everybody thought I'd gone completely nuts and was by now totally bonkers! I even went to speak with a taxidermist who quoted £10,000 to do Boxy. I thought it was a great idea. Why not? You see other animals and birds that way, and they were obviously once living creatures.

I pictured him standing at the edge of the shed, looking over on the herd, and most importantly for me, still here! I even talked about having him on wheels, wheeling him into a trailer, taking him to the Great Yorkshire Show and having him outside the Blonde Society marquee. I could have taken him to schools and schoolchildren who would then have seen just how good he looked. I still think it was a sensible idea.

Andrew thought £10,000 and the idea was stupid. We settled on cremation and began putting everything in place for the day.

I spoke with Phil Lord. Phil is a local knackerman and was involved as well as Jonathan from Bishopton.

The plan for 30 January 2018, the date we had booked, was that Jonathan would come and sedate Boxy, the deed would be done and Phil would take him for cremation. We would then receive Boxy's ashes.

Every time I went out to the shed, in between making the decision and the day itself, I kept thinking, 'He's alright, maybe I'm making the wrong decision.'

It was horrible really. When Christmas came, I couldn't help but think this was Boxy's last Christmas. My last Christmas with him.

I was trying to convince myself I was doing the right thing, but I was coming back more to the conclusion I wasn't! Why was I even thinking of ending his life when he was alright? Perhaps for me, I thought it might have been easier to have found him in the field. It was the planning for it, that was the bit that was so hard. It just didn't feel right.

The day before it was all due to take place everybody gave me a wide berth. I really wasn't in a good place, but strangely my night's sleep brought my best dream ever.

I was in the kitchen and there were a couple of cows tied up in there with me. I remember thinking that I don't normally have cows there, but there they were. As I looked out of the window up the hill there were some cows in the field and I saw Boxy running towards them.

I thought, 'Oh bugger, how am I going to get him back in?' And with that another big white bull appeared and that scared me because they would have fought and killed each other!

That's when I set off running up the hill, telling them off and shouting at them to stop fighting. It was all a bit weird because that wouldn't work – but it did!

They stopped fighting. I told Boxy to get himself back down to the house and we both came back in together.

When we reached the kitchen Boxy changed into a man. He was stood towering over me and began to talk.

My favourite part of Boxy were the curls on his face and cheeks, I used to love rubbing them, and this man's facial hair was Boxy's curls. As he was talking I just wanted to touch his face.

He told me it was the right time, that he was ready and that I had to let him go.

When I woke up it still felt real and right, and I was okay about what was to happen. I told Andrew I was okay about it all and when I went over to the shed to see Boxy that morning I could see it in his eyes. He was the man I'd seen. It was him. Boxy was looking at me in the way that was saying, 'Yeah, it were me, I'm ready.' It all made everything easier for me. It was almost as though the decision was now his, not mine.

Andrew and I had decided to put Boxy in the calving pen, separate from the rest of the herd but still by their side. I spent pretty much all day with him, sitting at his head, stroking him. He stayed laid down in his straw bedding all day. He wasn't ill, apart from his arthritis. He was comfortable, cosy and chilled out snacking on silage – an old gentleman and granddad.

As the time came closer I became upset again and couldn't help myself but cry. Boxy threw his head towards me, snorting and shaking his head. He'd never done that with me before in his whole life and I thought he wanted me to clear off, so that's what I did.

I went for a walk along the bridle path, had a good cry, drinking whisky in little sips from my hip flask and got myself back together. I then interpreted that Boxy couldn't cope with me being upset around him. He was used to me telling him everything was going to be alright and encouraging.

Mum and Dad came over and went to say their goodbyes to Boxy. Paul arrived, then Jonathan and Phil.

Andrew and I had formulated a plan to make sure Boxy and the rest of the herd weren't spooked. Whenever a knackerman comes the cattle smell the wagon and get a bit on edge. We had been adamant that we didn't want Phil to drive his wagon to the shed, so he parked it up near the house.

Jonathan and Andrew then walked from the house to the shed. Andrew slipped Boxy's halter on him and tied him to the front rails. Boxy just stood there. Jonathan injected the sedation into his rump. There was no drama. Jonathan came back to the house saying Boxy had been great. He went back over a short while later to check on how the sedation was going and came back saying Boxy was really sleepy and laid like a dog with his head resting on the floor.

Phil, Jonathan, Andrew, Paul and Dad all went over to see Boxy put to sleep. I put on my earphones and focused on my meditational recordings.

I was ready. I was calm. I was okay.

Then I heard it! The gun. Somehow, being inside and listening to the meditation sounds I hadn't anticipated hearing it, which was a bit stupid.

I screamed and burst into tears saying I didn't think I'd hear it, I didn't think I'd hear it, over and over again. Mum grabbed hold of me and held me tight.

Everybody came back in apart from Andrew, who was checking that everything would be okay when I came out and that the rest of the herd was okay, but he said they were all really calm. Normally, if an animal has to be put to sleep there is also usually a little blood and the smell of it gets the others hyped up, but they didn't.

'Boxy had got up when the time had come. He'd walked towards us. He'd stood perfectly still. It was all done very respectfully, causing the least amount of stress.'
Andrew McNeil

Jonathan had been a part of our journey throughout Boxy's life. He'd always been there when Boxy needed him and I hugged him afterwards, thanked him and wouldn't let go of him for what seemed a long time. Paul had gone over to make sure Andrew was okay. I think he just needed some time by himself, after all Boxy was a huge part of his life too.

I polished off the whisky and then spent most of that night laid on the settee with Dad at one end and my head on him – and sobbed.

After ten years of extreme highs and lows, successes, overcoming every hurdle put in his way, it was over. Boxy was gone. I felt a bit crap the next day, possibly more on account of the whisky I had drunk to get me through, but everyone, most of all Andrew, had done everything they could to protect me.

Everyone had known just how much Boxy had meant and still does mean to me.

I had spoken with Sue (Wilson) every day, and during the

whole of this time leading up to the day itself sometimes several times. I asked Sue to put into words here, the way she saw it for me during this time:

'Kate would ring maybe two or three times a day. She would ring, say, 'Hello, it's me,' and then burst out crying. It was raw, still is today and always will be.

'We speak every single day, but this was so important to her as she looked for the best way to end Boxy's life. She said all she wanted was for it to be the kindest way for him. She said he would know what she was thinking when she saw him and that when he looked at her he saw right into her soul.

'Boxy wasn't just an animal, or just a bull. He was part of Kate and what she was going through still brings tears to my eyes thinking about it.

'Boxy and Kate had a connection that I doubt I will ever see again and in all my years of being with animals it was the most incredible relationship I have ever witnessed.

'Just imagine a bull that has been in a pen on his own for nearly two years. I think about this a lot. Sometimes, in bad weather, he'd be up to his knees in puddles. This bull is a blooming working animal who knows what his game is. He's a big lad with immense strength and he's been there all this time. Then the day comes when he is about to be released and Kate puts him on a halter in front of a lot of people he's not seen before and they're having their pictures taken. Kate then calmly walks him into the field and lets him go.

'If that had been one of my bulls, I'd have been like a kite on the end of that lead. They had trust in each other, she in him and him in her.

'Kate was very up and down as she tried coming up with the best solution. It was heartbreaking for her, cruel having to let go, it was like she was cutting off half of herself.

'We talked and talked. I tried to keep her as level as I could because if she had been hit by her fibromyalgia that would have been the end of it. She wouldn't have been able to cope.

'Once she had come to terms with the way she was going to see it

through she became what I term clinical about it. It's the only way she knew how to handle the emotional side.

'I know how it feels to lose an animal that has been close to you, but I've never had a bond like Kate and Boxy's. I'm as soft as a kitten and I've just read the opening of this book and my eyes are already filled with tears and about to have a good cry as I know how heart-wrenching this time was for Kate.

'As long as she lives I think what she and Andrew had to do will still remain raw.'
Sue Wilson

Thank you so much Sue. Talk again tomorrow!

Chapter 54

The Show Season
That Never Was

We were all set to return to the show rings in the summer of 2018. We had a bull called Nugget and possibly some females, but we were really busy with Andrew's work, which also involves me on the embroidery side of the sports clothing.

We'd had a good run at the shows in the past three years and would have continued, even though summer is our busiest time for the clothing and embroidery business and it's when all the shows take place.

We knew how tired we would be come the end of the season, as there is so much to do feeding and bedding the animals that don't go to a show, morning and night, as well as the preparatory work before a show and getting back and unloading afterwards for those that do. It's not a complaint. Everyone has to do it.

Lincolnshire Show was to be Nugget's debut as a young bull and we had high hopes, as usual, but we never got there and we haven't shown since!

We were all packed up and ready to go on the Monday evening before the show when we received a call from a lady who wanted to come and look at our bulls. We told her we only had one for sale and he was bound for the show.

The lady asked whether she could come the next morning, so we altered our plans and decided we would go to the show in the afternoon, as the show starts on a Wednesday.

Nugget, who was just 13 months old, was bought, loaded up

on the lady's truck and away he went.

Andrew and I stood in the yard and decided that was it, we weren't going to show. We had already sold the rest of our other youngstock we'd intended to sell in between Boxy going and the Lincolnshire Show. McAlan and McKendall had gone for breeding. We really didn't have anything we were wanting to show.

We still went to the Lincolnshire, as spectators, and really enjoyed it. We had nothing left to show or sell at that time. That summer we realised that with Andrew's business going so well we didn't miss the showing side. We still went to some of them, but purely as a day out.

That's when we made the decision to go for High Health status. I was always selective where I tied our cattle at shows, with no noticeable contact with other animals from other herds. I'd always been conscious of breed health, and high health status is now one of the major selling points in pedigree livestock.

Andrew is quite academic. He likes to learn and understands about EBV figures, which bore me, but I know they are important for success in breeding. I just like to get out and be with the animals. It's the farmer in me. We work together really well.

'Our high health status is very important to us. You've to tick a lot of boxes. Showing is something we enjoy and have enjoyed. We've now had a lot of success without showing, selling predominantly to other pedigree herds. All of our females go that way while the bulls go to both pedigree and suckler herds. Our cattle all have a good temperament and we ensure they are going to good homes. We have been directly responsible, supplying our stock, for several new pedigree herds.'
Andrew McNeil

Not going to shows and being a closed herd increase the health status of our herd because there is less chance of cattle contracting disease or illness. And, as Andrew said, our trade has increased because of the reputation of our animals through our earlier showing and our annual breeding programme.

I thought I would miss not showing for a second year in 2019, especially the Great Yorkshire Show, but I didn't and then of course last year in 2020 it didn't take place at all, because of Covid. At the time of writing this in April 2021 we still have no great plans to show, but who knows?

Sales are going well, we have a lovely place and a great herd. We're not saying never again to showing.

There was a quote published in the *Yorkshire Post* in 2016 where I said: 'I want other breeders to come and say that's the ten best pedigree Blondes I've ever seen. It's not about the money, it's about being known for breeding quality, being accepted as a serious breeder and sitting out on a summer's evening watching the herd grazing.'

I still feel the same today.

The Bull That Lives On

Boxy and Dora's influence is still in our herd. Dora gave birth to her eleventh calf earlier this year (2021) – StevieGee – a bull calf, after two previous heifer calves Precious and Origin.

We currently have ten breeding females and one working bull, Katem Orsum, who is a Boxster grandson. We still have Jewel and Justice, our first two Katem heifer calves and they will be here forever. Fern, who was also very special to us, has gone to Sue up at Burnt Yates where she is looked after royally.

Boxy's semen is ensuring that his legend lives on all around the world. There are currently 75 pedigree cows on the Blonde database, in several countries, who have been artificially inseminated with Boxy and have carried his progeny. Dad is back using Boxy's semen in his herd once again. Boxy is on the UK Sires Elite Beef Breeding List. Our herd is made up of his daughters, granddaughters and grandsons.

And I got my wish! Boxy was in the house with me for a short while, but not quite as he appeared in that dream.

We actually got his ashes back a few weeks after he was put to sleep but kept them in the house beside my chair till I was ready to move him. On my birthday it felt the right time.

Andrew then made a shelf and Boxy's ashes are in what was Alan Hall's show box in the cattle shed. Highly appropriate, since Alan bred him. Boxy's still here, in that box, on the shelf, looking over the herd. Phil had also taken a lock of his hair and had had it framed for me. He understood just how special this bull was.

I have an engraved bracelet, a gold copy of his ear tag and number and never take it off! Mum and I had a lot of jewellery that had been of sentimental value to me melted down to have it made.

It's very special. I feel like I have a piece of him with me all the time and it reminds me that I have the strength to achieve anything I truly believe in regardless of the odds.

We had such times together. We had such a bond. I cannot see ever having that again with any other animal. I can see Boxy in my mind and he's with me wherever I go. He never lost, whether in the show ring, in the High Court or in the hearts of others throughout the UK and abroad. Without Boxy, Andrew and I would not be at Wrancarr Mill. We would not have won so much in the show rings, we would not have the reputation our stock has earned us, we would not have met so many wonderful people.

Do I miss him? Oh God, yeah, every day. He was some special boy!

We had and have a love that will never die – Boxy lives on!

NOTES FROM THE JUDGMENT MADE BY THE HONOURABLE MR. JUSTICE McCOMBE:

The following are extracts from the 'APPROVED JUDGMENT':

My finding is that Boxster's samples were mixed on site. My reasons are as follows.

The witnesses who gave evidence on this issue were Mrs Catherine McNeil, (the daughter of Mr Kendall Jackson and Mrs Anita Jackson, the owners of the farm), Mr and Mrs Jackson themselves, Mr Melvin Burrows and Mr John Davison, on behalf of Jacksons and Beyonce and Britney on behalf of DEFRA.

I am satisfied that the account given by Jacksons' witnesses is to be preferred to that given by Beyonce and Britney.

First, in the absence of deliberate dishonesty on the part of Jacksons' witnesses, and none is alleged, it seems to me to be impossible to find that all of them were mistaken on the simple point about where the animals in issue, all well known to them, were tethered for the testing process and where they themselves were at the important moments. All these witnesses were well acquainted with their animals and can hardly have been mistaken as to which was placed where. This was also a significant day for these witnesses; their herd had never been tested in this way before. On the other hand neither Beyonce nor Britney had any previous acquaintance with any of the Jacksons' animals and had carried out testing procedures on many other farms. The possibility of them being mistaken about a simple matter, such as the positioning of the animals, and where the staff were standing, is far more likely.

Secondly, it seems to me inconsistent with all the evidence that Beyonce should have been told, as she says in her statement, that all three of the animals tethered together at the top of the yard were calm and unlikely to pose problems if one of them had in fact been Vinnie. It is common ground that Vinnie was known to all not to like needles and that Beyonce was informed of this.

Thirdly, the positioning of the animals as Jacksons contend is supported by other features. Boxster and Katie were being kept deliberately segregated from the rest of the herd and Jacksons would have been, and were in fact, anxious to demonstrate that, particularly in the presence of DEFRA representatives. It also seems likely that Katie, Boxster's constant companion, would be tested with him and at the same time so that the two animals could then be removed together back to the isolation pen, as Jacksons say they were. It seems odd that Katie would be left to be tested separately from Boxster, in the crush with other animals as DEFRA's witnesses would have it. Mr Jackson also gave cogent evidence that it was very unwise to tether together, during testing, two mature bulls, one of which (Vinnie) was notoriously unhappy with needles. That evidence made obvious common sense.

Fourthly, the account now given by DEFRA's witnesses is inconsistent with the first account given to Miss Clare Taylor on 3 June 2010 and noted by her in her diary. The note indicates that it was the *second* bull that caused difficulties while the first caused no problems. Now the witnesses say that the first bull tested was Vinnie and that it was he who played up. Further, that note makes no mention of names whereas the evidence now is that the technicians knew the names of the animals from the outset. This is not what their own written reports to Miss Clare Taylor reflect.

I refused an application by DEFRA to adduce further written or oral evidence from Miss Clare Taylor as to the circumstances in which her note was compiled. This was for two reasons. First, this went beyond the confines of the order made for cross-examination of witnesses. Secondly, and most importantly, it seemed to me to be unfair to permit DEFRA to attempt to retrieve in this manner a weakness in its own witnesses' evidence exposed in cross-examination on the previous day.

Fifthly, Britney was, I thought, an unreliable witness in her account of how her own note of the events had been compiled. It was put to her that from her position at the time she could not have seen what happened when Boxster was tested. She said that while she could not see the needle inserted, she could 'see the action'; she could see him move but could not see blood going into the tube. She assumed that when the needle was inserted the bull jumped. She could not see the needle inserted or withdrawn or the vacuum in the tube being lost.

She went on to say that she did not discuss what happened with Beyonce before giving her own account; she was, she said, merely setting out normal testing procedure. She was then reminded of Miss Clare Taylor's note of 3 June 2010 and acknowledged that she had been sitting in Miss Clare Taylor's office, listening on the loudspeaker phone, when Beyonce was questioned about the matter on that day. She then said that not all aspects of the incident had been covered in that conversation which was only brief. She continued to insist that she had not heard Beyonce's account before compiling her own note, notwithstanding the shared telephone conversation on 3 June. I do not accept her evidence on this point.

It was pointed out to her further that her note said that, owing to Vinnie's reaction, it had been decided to get his sample 'when the animal was in a crush' whereas Mr Jackson's evidence was that Vinnie was too large for the crush. She then said, as Beyonce had said in her note, that Vinnie was tested 'behind a gate in the penning area'. None of this was satisfactory and conflicted with other evidence.

This aspect of DEFRA's case brought me to the conclusion that it was in the case of DEFRA's witnesses, rather than that of Jacksons' witnesses, that a received 'orthodoxy' had crept into the accounts, impairing the reliability of the evidence given.

Sixthly, I prefer the inference drawn from the sampling sheets advanced by Mr Stilitz to that which Miss Anderson invites, namely that the missing 1054 vial is to be accounted for in the manner contended by the Jacksons. The contrary explanation of the missing tube having been in Beyonce's pocket appears to have been speculation after the event, unsupported by her own and Britney's contemporaneous accounts.

While the technicians' attitudes to recommended procedures seems clearly to have been casual and while this part of the written procedures may have been referable to a period before bar coding, it seems odd that spares for the pocket should be taken from the middle of a sequence, thus needlessly interrupting it contrary to the instructions, rather than from some remote part of the collection where the sequence would not be impaired.

Miss Anderson argued that the laboratory testing of Boxster's sample revealed no contamination which she submitted would have been inevitable if the scientific evidence adduced by Jacksons is correct. However, it is disputed whether contamination would in fact have been detected by the controls. That dispute is not amenable to resolution on the evidence available, particularly in the absence of cross-examination of the scientists. Neither party asked for such cross-examination at any stage. It was not apparently suggested at the time cross-examination was suggested by Mr Rabinder Singh QC, nor indeed was it suggested before me on the first day of the hearing, when the matter was briefly re-argued, that this scientific evidence could be conclusive for or against a finding of mixing in the field. I therefore regard this aspect as neutral as the evidence presently stands.

The central issue in the case is not based upon a challenge to an error of material fact at all. It is a challenge of law based upon an allegation of breach of Jacksons' legitimate expectation…

… I do not think that the justice of the case, or the requirements of fairness, would be met by proceeding on the false assumption that the samples had not been mixed or that there was some unresolved doubt about it…

I conclude, therefore, that Mr Stilitz's submission is correct and that I should assess the legal challenge on the basis of the facts as I have found them to be.

The question then arises whether the mixing of Boxster's samples and the failure to conduct a re-test fell foul of the 'requirement of good administration, by which public bodies ought to deal straightforwardly and consistently with the public'.

... It seems to me that any natural reading would be that any flaw in the testing process from sampling on the farm to laboratory work would lead to a re-test. That accords too with common sense. Most would think that, if it is shown that any part of this process had not been properly carried out in accordance with good practice, a re-test would follow out of an abundance of caution, particularly where the practice is said to have been adopted to guard against contamination. As a matter of ordinary understanding, it would be taken that such a flaw, whether detected before or after the conclusion of the laboratory testing process, might lead either to a false positive or a false negative result; either would be seen by the reasonable observer as undesirable and a re-test would be the natural expectation.

So far in the argument, therefore, I consider that it is made out that DEFRA has fallen foul of the principle of good administration...

Jacksons' desire has always been for Boxster to be re-tested and have offered to meet the cost of so doing. In granting the initial injunction in the proceedings in Jacksons' favour on 24 August 2010, Collins J advanced this as the 'sensible course'. That was obviously the sensible course then and it is surprising that it was not taken...

I conclude that this application for judicial review should be granted for the reasons set out above...

I would propose, therefore, to quash the decisions to issue the statutory notices and the notices themselves (dated 13 April and 29 July 2010). Subject to further argument, I would also consider making an appropriate declaration (in a form to be settled) that the presence of bTB has not been 'officially established' in this animal within the meaning of Article 15 of the Directive.

I do not consider it to be appropriate to make a mandatory order for re-testing. The question of what are the appropriate steps now is, in my view, a matter for DEFRA, in the light of all that has happened, including the diverging opinions on the science that have come before this court and which it has not been possible to resolve. Obviously, in the light of all that has been discussed in this case, re-testing, by any or all of the means discussed, should be seriously considered as one of the options open and should not be rejected out of hand, as it has been to date, simply because DEFRA's witnesses in the case have argued for the rejection of that option. It seems to me that it would be desirable for these reasons that any further decision is made by officials not previously involved with the present case.

Yard layout and cattle locations

/ = Gates ⬭ = Cattle tied up 1 Nectarine, 2 Boxster, 3 Katie, 4, other Pedigree 5, other Pedigree 6, Vi (big cow) 7, Vinnie

All dividing walls are not permanent and can be moved to accommodate the size of the group.

Shelved area for the safe use/ storage of equipment

Crush Pen

Empty (used to send cattle out into the crush) each group moved into here before being driven into the crush for safety reasons. Animals are always contained.

Cow & Calves in pen

Path cattle take through crush before returning to their pen

Fattening Cattle in pen

Pedigree Bulls in pen

Pedigree Heifers in pen

3 Large Pedigree Bulls in pen

Farm House

Entrance to cattle yard.

Wood Yard